Somme 1916

# British Infantryman
## VERSUS
# German Infantryman

Stephen Bull

First published in Great Britain in 2014 by Osprey Publishing,
PO Box 883, Oxford, OX1 9PL, UK
PO Box 3985, New York, NY 10185-3985, USA
E-mail: info@ospreypublishing.com

Osprey Publishing is part of the Osprey Group

A CIP catalogue record for this book is available from the
British Library

Print ISBN: 978 1 78200 914 6
PDF ebook ISBN: 978 1 78200 916 0
ePub ebook ISBN: 978 1 78200 915 3

Index by Marie-Pierre Evans
Typeset in Univers, Sabon and Adobe Garamond Pro
Maps by bounford.com
Originated by PDQ Media, Bungay, UK
Printed in China through Asia Pacific Offset Ltd

14 15 16 17 18  10 9 8 7 6 5 4 3 2 1

Osprey Publishing is supporting the Woodland Trust, the UK's
leading woodland conservation charity, by funding the dedication
of trees.

www.ospreypublishing.com

## Author's acknowledgements

Thanks are due to the Imperial War Museum London (IWM),
The National Archives (TNA) and the North West Sound Archive
(NWSA), which hold many of the first-hand documents and
recordings used in the writing of this account. Also to Garry
Smith, Curator of the Manchester Regiment Museum, members
of the Manchester Regiment forum, Colonel Mike Glover,
The Fusilier Museum, Bury, and to Jane Davies of The Duke
of Lancaster's Regiment Museum, Fulwood. Special mention
must also be made of Fergus Read, who worked with the late
Bill Turner in his groundbreaking research on the Accrington
Pals, Andrew Jackson, Martin Pegler and of Professor Gerhard
Hirschfeld of Stuttgart. The photographs are from the author's
collection, unless otherwise specified.

## Artist's note

Readers may care to note that the original paintings from which
the plates of this book were prepared are available for private
sale. All reproduction copyright whatsoever is retained by the
Publishers. All enquiries should be addressed to:

Peter Dennis, 'Fieldhead', The Park, Mansfield, Nottinghamshire
NG18 2AT, UK, or email magie.h@ntlworld.com

The Publishers regret that they can enter into no correspondence
upon this matter.

## Editor's note

For ease of comparison please refer to the following conversion
table:
1 mile = 1.6km
1yd = 0.9m
1ft = 0.3m
1in = 2.54cm/25.4mm
1lb = 0.45kg

## Comparative officer ranks

| British | British abbrev. | German |
|---|---|---|
| colonel | Col | Oberst |
| lieutenant-colonel | Lt-Col | Oberstleutnant |
| major | Maj | Major |
| captain | Capt | Hauptmann |
| lieutenant | Lt | Oberleutnant |
| 2nd lieutenant | 2/Lt | Leutnant |
| no equivalent ('sergeant-major lieutenant') | | Feldwebelleutnant |
| no equivalent ('deputy officer') | | Offizierstellvertreter |
| regimental sergeant-major | RSM | Etatmässige Feldwebel |
| company sergeant-major | CSM | Feldwebel |
| no equivalent ('junior company sergeant-major') | | Vizefeldwebel |
| no equivalent ('ensign') | | Fähnrich |
| sergeant | Sgt | Sergeant |
| corporal | Cpl | Unteroffizier |
| lance corporal | L/Cpl | Gefreiter |
| private | Pte | Soldat/Musketier/Grenadier, etc. |

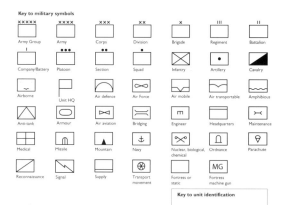

# CONTENTS

# Introduction

'My eyes swept the valley – long lines of men, officers at their head in the half crouching attitude which modern tactics dictate, resembling suppliants rather than the vanguard of a great offensive, were moving forward over three miles of front,' recalled Capt G.S. Hutchinson, 33rd Battalion, Machine Gun Corps, of the events of 15 July 1916.

Heavily laden Northumberland Fusiliers of 103rd (Tyneside Irish) Brigade, 34th (New Army) Division, attacking at La Boisselle on 1 July 1916. L/Cpl Will Marshall, who went over the top with 11th East Lancashire's fourth wave on 1 July, would later recall that between soldiers a dispersion of 'about two yards apart' was maintained (NWSA). Recent research suggests that in the event it was a minority rather than a majority of British units that adhered to rigid lines and set tempo on 1 July. However, how fast the attacking infantry ought to have moved remains an open question, since to arrive in front of an enemy position winded and unable to fight would have been highly undesirable. This was the situation that British doctrine attempted to avoid, on the premise that real action would commence only after the German front line had been reached.

As the attackers rose, white bursts of shrapnel appeared among the trees and thinly across the ridge towards Martinpuich … Two, three, possibly four, seconds later an inferno of rifle and machine gun fire broke from the edge of High Wood, from high up in its trees, and from all along the ridge to the village. The line staggered. Men fell forward limply and quietly. The hiss and crack of bullets filled the air and skimmed the long grasses … Some two hundred men, their commander at their head, had been brought to a standstill at this point. A scythe seemed to cut their feet from under them, and the line crumpled and fell, stricken by machine gun fire. Those in support wavered, then turned to fly. There was no shred of cover and they fell in their tracks. (Quoted in Powell 2006: 70–71)

The battle of the Somme was barely a century ago and many eyewitness accounts remain: yet few historical events are so lapped about with myth, or arouse such trenchant opinions regarding its significance, its tactics, its objectives and its leading characters. For the British, the Somme was shocking not just for its scale and modernity, but because for the first time it committed the essentially citizen 'New Armies' to massed combat in the main theatre of war, against the main enemy. For the Germans, the Entente attack came as a kind of relief after many days of intensive bombardment, as Unteroffizier Otto Lais recalled:

> No longer must we calm, hold down, tie down those men who almost lose their minds through this pounding, booming and splintering, through difficulty in breathing and through the jerking and swaying of the dugout walls, and who with overtly trembling limbs want to get up away from this hole and this mousetrap, up into the open air, into a landscape of raging flames and iron – a landscape of insanity and death. (Lais 1935)

Whether the assault on the Somme was a serious attempt at a major Entente breakthrough, or a phase of a 'wearing out' battle, remains a matter of debate.

Though posed in a mine crater as early as June 1916, this photograph gives a good impression of how counter-attacking German troops were equipped for the Somme battlefield. Armed with rifles and grenades, most are wearing the 1915-type gas mask. As gas was an unpredictable area weapon, often injuring and debilitating rather than killing outright, swift, effective protection was vital. By mid-1916 gas warfare technology was advancing rapidly, if unevenly: how best to deliver gas was still a live debate, and wind and weather were never entirely overcome.

The 18-pdr field gun, standard weapon of the British field artillery. Capable of a dozen rounds a minute, it was ideal for firing air-bursting shrapnel shells against targets in the open. It could also fire high explosive but was of marginal use against bunkers and obstacle zones.

The idea for a major Franco-British offensive in 1916 dated back to December 1915. General Sir Douglas Haig took command of the British Expeditionary Force on 19 December, and following authorization from the prime minister he began planning with the French, whom it was originally intended should play the biggest part. By early in the New Year it was decided that the attack would be astride the River Somme, with a provisional start date of 1 August. All this was suddenly upset, when, on 21 February the German Army chief of staff, General der Infanterie Erich von Falkenhayn, opened the major German offensive against the French at Verdun. In the face of initial German success Haig was forced to assume responsibility for planning the attack on the Somme, while French participation was scaled back, and there were calls for the date to be brought forward.

Finally, a scheme emerged in which the opening of the main attack would comprise 13 British divisions to the north and 11 French to the south. For the British, the 'first objective' was the Pozières Ridge, followed by either a turn to the north to roll up the enemy line, or outright breakthrough, exploited by cavalry. By way of diversion, the village of Gommecourt would also be attacked. Huge mines would blow out critical points in the enemy line, but cornerstone to all was the artillery bombardment planned by Maj-Gen Noel Birch, originally intended to last five days, but extended owing to bad weather. This was to use 1,537 guns on the British front alone to work over enemy trenches, billets, batteries and communications, as well as to cut

belts of wire. Each morning began with a concerted 80 minutes, except on the last morning when after 65 minutes the barrage would lift from the German front line.

Though hugely impressive, the Entente artillery plan would fail in several respects. There were too few heavy guns to deal with deep bunkers; wire was cut only in places; and many German batteries, kept silent as long as possible, survived to open up on the attackers. Moreover, the long bombardment – though it killed, injured, stunned or demoralized many – gave away whatever remained of secrecy and surprise. That there would be a major offensive had been published in the Allied press; exactly where, and approximately when, was announced by the guns.

The plan for General der Infanterie Fritz von Below's 2. Armee on the hitherto quiet Somme sector was essentially defensive. The German front would be held in modest strength, with heavy reliance on fixed defences and artillery pre-registered on points of potential threat. Close protection of the trench lines fell mainly to thick belts of wire, and machine guns, positioned as far as possible to avoid detection and enfilade the front. Local counter-attack could deal with incursions. At the outset five divisions were deployed north of the Somme, three to the south, and three in reserve. With German offensive activity focused on Verdun, much would depend on whether 2. Armee could withstand the initial onslaught, and what reserves would be brought in as the battle of the Somme unfolded.

Drummers of Reserve-Infanterie-Regiment Nr. 55. This Westphalian unit fought with distinction in the Gommecourt sector as part of 2. Garde-Reserve-Division, launching counter-attacks even on the first day. Over the ensuing ten weeks the regiment was gradually ground down until companies averaged 130 to 140 men each (theoretically, wartime strength was five officers and 260 other ranks): it was finally dislodged from Beaucourt-sur-l'Ancre toward the end of the battle. These men wear the *Bluse*, a fly-fronted garment introduced in late 1915 as a practical and economic alternative to the existing tunic. The *Bluse* is teamed with *Marschstiefel* (jackboots), field cap and leather belt with Prussian buckle.

**MAP KEY**

**1  1–13 July**: The battle of Albert. General Sir Henry Rawlinson's Fourth Army – of which fully 12 divisions, grouped in four corps, will fight on the first day – mounts the initial 'Big Push' against German forces of General der Infanterie Fritz Below's 2. Armee. As part of 31st Division, opposite Serre, 11th East Lancashire takes part in the 1 July attack, against elements of Infanterie-Regiment Nr. 169 (52. Division); 7th Bedfordshire (18th (Eastern) Division) and 18th Manchester (30th Division), opposite Montauban, and Infanterie-Regiment Nr. 180 (26. Reserve-Division), at Thiepval, also participate. The attack results in total failure for the British forces in the north, including the diversionary attack on Gommecourt, put in by two divisions of General Sir Edmund Allenby's Third Army. In concert with the French, there is some advance in the south around Mametz and Montauban, but over two weeks the battle degenerates into numerous small assaults, culminating in British attacks on Mametz and Trônes woods; the former was finally captured on 12 July, but the latter would fall to the British only on the 14th.

**2  14–17 July:** The battle of Bazentin Ridge. As General Sir Hubert Gough's Reserve Army takes over responsibility for the northern sector the Entente offensive refocuses on the south, beginning with a short, intensive bombardment. The British mount a well-executed night attack and penetrate the German second position, but the attackers stall in the face of stubborn German resistance around Pozières, Longueval and Guillemont. British cavalry deployment at High Wood proves premature.

**3  14 July–3 September:** The battle of Delville Wood. In an attempt to straighten the front and secure the British right flank, British and Empire forces attack Delville Wood, Longueval and Trônes Wood. The South African Brigade, serving with 9th (Scottish) Division, is committed and suffers appalling losses; the Germans make repeated counter-attacks, and are only driven from the wood on 3 September. British attempts to take Guillemont – including the 30 July attack in which 18th Manchester and Reserve-Infanterie-Regiment Nr. 104 (24. Reserve-Division) are involved – fail. On 19 July a subsidiary attack is mounted by two divisions of General Sir Charles Monro's First Army at Fromelles to the north, but fails entirely. Also on 19 July, the Germans reorganize their command structure, with a new 1. Armee created under the Below's command; General der Infanterie Max von Gallwitz is appointed 2. Armee commander but also commands a new parent formation, Heeresgruppe Gallwitz, intended to co-ordinate the actions of the two German armies on the Somme. Further changes at a senior level occur on 29 August, as Generalfeldmarschall Paul von Hindenburg replaces General der Infanterie Erich von Falkenhayn as the German Army's chief of staff.

**4  20–25 July:** Subsidiary British attacks at High Wood prove unsuccessful; it falls only on 15 September.

**5  23 July–3 September:** The battle of Pozières Ridge. Combined Australian and British efforts eventually succeed in securing Pozières, in the teeth of numerous German counter-attacks.

**6  3–6 September:** The battle of Guillemont. After many unsuccessful attempts Guillemont is finally taken by Entente forces.

**7  9 September:** The battle of Ginchy. With Guillemont now secure, 16th (Irish) Division takes Ginchy at the first attempt.

**8  15–22 September:** The battle of Flers-Courcelette. The Mark I tank makes its first appearance in support of an attempted British, Canadian and New Zealand breakthrough at Flers, Martinpuich and Courcelette. Despite Entente advances of more than a mile, there is no breakthrough. On 21 September, Hindenburg orders that the Somme sector be given priority for troops and supplies; two days later, the Germans begin work on a rear defensive line, the Siegfriedstellung, known as the Hindenburg Line to the British.

**9  25–28 September:** The battle of Morval. In concert with the French, Fourth Army puts in attacks at Morval, Gueudecourt and Lesbœufs, all of which are captured.

**10  26–28 September:** The battle of Thiepval Ridge. British and Canadian troops of Gough's Reserve Army – including 7th Bedfordshire – pinch off the Thiepval salient, and capture German positions on high ground that have resisted attack since 1 July. Infanterie-Regiment Nr. 180, having defended Thiepval on 1 July and thereafter, is finally dislodged from the village. By 28 September Prince Rupprecht, the German army group commander, has no reserves left in the Somme sector.

**11  1–18 October:** The battle of the Transloy Ridges. Fourth Army is now confronted by a fourth line of German defences, behind which further lines are under construction. Le Sars is taken by the British, but bad weather sets in.

**12  1 October–11 November:** The battle of the Ancre Heights. Gough's Reserve Army, now named Fifth Army, slowly works forward. German counter-attacks fail, their reinforcements dwindling as the French re-open operations at Verdun.

**13  13–18 November:** The battle of the Ancre. Following heavy bombardment, Fifth Army takes Beaumont-Hamel, Saint-Pierre Divion and Beaucourt-sur-l'Ancre. Serre, still garrisoned by Infanterie-Regiment Nr. 169 and other elements of 52. Division, remains in German hands. In early 1917 the Germans successfully withdraw to the Hindenburg Line.

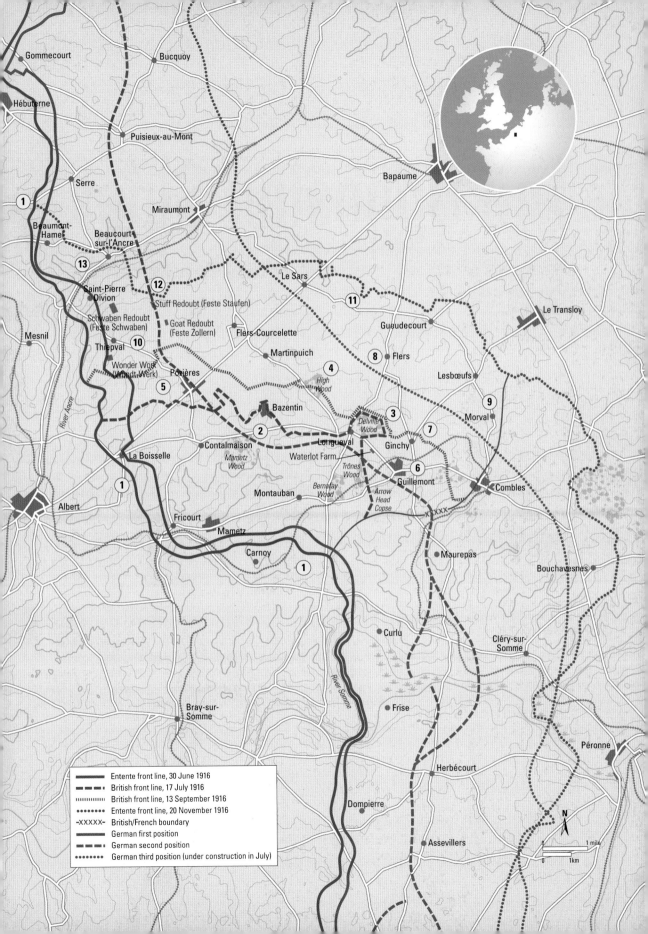

Gommecourt

Bucquoy

Bapaume

Hébuterne

Puisieux-au-Mont

Serre

(1)

Miraumont

Le Transloy

Beaumont-
Hamel

Beaucourt
sur-l'Ancre

Le Sars

(11)

(13)

(12)

Stuff Redoubt (Feste Staufen)

Gueudecourt

Saint-Pierre
Divion

Schwaben Redoubt
(Feste Schwaben)

Goat Redoubt
(Feste Zollern)

Flers-Courcelette

(8) Flers

Mesnil

Thiepval

(10)

Martinpuich

Lesbœufs

Wonder Work
(Wundt-Werk)

Pozières

(5)

(4)

High
Wood

(9)

Morval

Bazentin

(2)

Delville
Wood

(3)

(7)

La Boisselle

Contalmaison

Longueval

Ginchy

Mametz
Wood

Waterlot Farm

Trônes
Wood

(6)

Guillemont

Combles

(1)

Montauban

Bernafay
Wood

Albert

Fricourt

Arrow
Head
Copse

XXXX

Mametz

Maurepas

Carnoy

Bouchavesnes

(1)

Curlu

Cléry-sur-
Somme

River Ancre

River Somme

Frise

Bray-sur-
Somme

Péronne

Herbécourt

N

Dompierre

Entente front line, 30 June 1916
British front line, 17 July 1916
British front line, 13 September 1916
Entente front line, 20 November 1916
-XXXXX- British/French boundary
German first position
German second position
German third position (under construction in July)

Assevillers

1 mile

1km

# The Opposing Sides

## ORIGINS AND RECRUITMENT

### British

Lord Kitchener of Khartoum (1850–1916). Unlike many others, he realized that continental commitment, and the possibility of a very long war, demanded a British Army different in quality and of vastly expanded size. Often circumventing the established channels of War Office and Territorial Associations, at the time of its inception 'Kitchener's Army' was a genuinely popular force. Kitchener did not live to see the 'New Army' divisions fight on the Somme; en route to Russia in June 1916 HMS *Hampshire* hit a mine and sank, taking with her Kitchener and most of the crew.

Though well trained, the British Army at the outbreak of World War I was modest in size, tempered to the needs of Empire, and second fiddle to the Royal Navy. In addition to six battalions of Foot Guards, its infantry comprised regiments, each generally consisting of two regular battalions, supplemented by one or two 'Militia' battalions providing a 'Special Reserve', and also one or more battalions of the 'Territorial Force', part-time soldiers who were not obliged to serve abroad and so would be called upon in 1914 to signify their willingness to go overseas on 'Imperial Service'. So it was, for example, that The Bedfordshire Regiment contained 1st and 2nd Regular battalions – 1st Battalion in Ireland and 2nd Battalion in South Africa when war was declared – plus 3rd (Reserve) Battalion, 4th (Extra Reserve) Battalion and 5th Battalion of the Territorial Force. The credit for the transformation of this small army into the largest ever fielded by Britain is now generally accorded to Field Marshal Horatio Herbert Kitchener, Victorian war hero, called to the cabinet as Secretary of State for War at the outbreak of the conflict.

At first the British Expeditionary Force to the Continent was essentially Regular, topped off with Reservists; those Territorials who had signified themselves willing to undertake 'Imperial Service' soon followed on. By 1916, however, the influx to the Western Front was increasingly of 'Kitchener men'. During the early stages of the Somme offensive, no fewer than 18 of the 25 divisions of General Sir Henry Rawlinson's Fourth Army were 'New Army', against just five Regular and two Territorial. Until the enlistment of new streams of conscripts in 1916 the Army was all volunteer, and composed to a significant extent of 'citizen soldiers'.

Intended to exist for three years, or the duration of the war, New Army units were designated 'Service' battalions. Professional men volunteered in droves and industrial regions were well represented, with particularly high enlistment in the Midlands, North, southern Scotland and London. Eventually, 557 New Army battalions were formed, of which 215 were raised by local committees who clothed, housed and fed them until they were formally adopted by the War Office in 1915. Leading light of recruitment through local committees was Edward G.V. Stanley, 17th Earl of Derby (1865–1948), Director-General of Recruiting and then Under-Secretary of State for War, who coined the term 'Pals'. While the popular picture of the Pals is that they were

Bantams, including a sergeant of The Lancashire Fusiliers, left, with tall Scottish sergeant for comparison. In total, 12 battalions of The Lancashire Fusiliers served on the Somme; three – 17th, 18th and 20th (Service) battalions, serving with 35th Division – were raised as Bantam units. Concentrated formations of short troops looked impressive, and may have been an enlistment and morale coup, but initial levels of fitness were not good.

friends drawn from the same streets and employment – as Derby had proposed in Liverpool in August 1914 – there was in fact considerable variety. For example, the unit that became the 'Accrington Pals' – or in official terms 11th (Service) Battalion (Accrington), The East Lancashire Regiment, or simply 11th East Lancashire – had its origin not in just one town but in four separate companies raised in Accrington, Burnley, Blackburn and Chorley, with other men drawn from Clayton-le-Moors, Great Harwood, Rishton, Church and Oswaldtwistle. In contrast, in Preston – where many had already been recruited into the other units, including the Territorials – the numbers of men raised by the local committee were never sufficient to create a Pals battalion, and those found were diverted into 7th (Service) Battalion, The Loyal North Lancashire Regiment.

Formed at Bedford in September 1914, the men of 7th Bedfordshire were not among the first of the Kitchener recruits, but nevertheless were a 'K2' battalion, all volunteers. Recruited mainly from Bedfordshire and Hertfordshire, the 'Shiny Seventh' Bedfordshire were quickly up to strength. Though first attached to 15th (Scottish) Division at Aldershot, the battalion was passed to 54th Infantry Brigade of 18th (Eastern) Division in May 1915, a 'second wave' formation destined to garner a considerable reputation.

With the slowing of recruitment, requirements were relaxed. Minimum height was first reduced from 5ft 3in to 5ft 0in, and subsequently 'Bantam' battalions including men as short as 4ft 10in were created. Nevertheless, while working-class recruits from Britain's industrial cities were often dubious physical specimens, they were balanced by the better-fed middle class, and countrymen. The Germans examined thousands of British prisoners captured on the Somme between July and November and analysed the age structure of the sample over time. In every month, between 50 and 60 per cent of the captives were in the 17–24 age group, with 33 to 43 per cent aged 25–35. Never did those older than 35 exceed 15 per cent of the bag. The conclusion was depressing: after two years of war the British Army still comprised 'a very high proportion of young and vigorous men'.

## German

The Deutsches Heer (German Army) of 1914 was arguably the most potent war machine in the world, and hitherto its reputation was of virtually unbroken success. Its bedrock was conscription: military duty to Kaiser and nation was broadly accepted as counterpoint to security and economic liberties, and military men enjoyed influence and respect. Prussia and the smaller states contributed 78 per cent of recruits; Bavaria 11; Saxony 7; and Württemberg 4 per cent. Liability for service commenced at 17 and continued until a citizen's 45th birthday. New classes of recruit were called to the musters yearly, medically examined and the numbers specified by statute enrolled into the Stehendes Heer (Standing Army). In the infantry, active service was supposed to be two years, followed by five years with the Reserve, 12 with the Landwehr (Territorial Army) and six with the Landsturm (Home Defence). Additionally, in times of need, 17- to 20-year-olds could also be inducted into the Landsturm. As the numbers needed in peacetime were lower than the males in the eligible age brackets, some were put into the Ersatz ('replacement' or 'supplementary') Reserve, and a *Restanten*, or remainder, were temporarily passed over. Conversely, some young men who wished to make a career of the Army might be admitted sooner, and there were *Einjährig-Freiwilligen* (one-year volunteers) who paid their own expenses and might later be regarded as suitable candidates to be officers of the Reserve.

Though it may be argued that the increasing industrialization and urbanization of Wilhelmine Germany did nothing to improve the fitness of the individual recruit, population increase, growing trade and mechanization did increase numbers available to the Army and provided the wherewithal with which they could be equipped and transported (Wurmb 1908: 32–43). Over a million men a year were processed by the recruitment machine, with 1,328,019 being called for examination in 1913 alone. Of these about half were actually required straight away, with 305,675 going to the Standing Army, 118,300 to the Landsturm, 86,911 to the Ersatz Reserve, and others to the Kaiserliche Marine (Imperial German Navy). Moreover, in the event of emergency, the recall of those who had passed from the Standing Army to the Reserve immediately swelled the ranks and embodied the Reserve regiments.

Efficient as the German system undoubtedly was, war and heavy losses tested it to its limits. In peacetime, recruits for the Standing Army were inducted at 20, but as conflict continued, call-up came progressively earlier. As a US translation of a French document of April 1917 explained, Reservists of all classes were called up during 1914, and many volunteers were also absorbed. Then in the first three months of 1915 came Landsturm men up to the age of 35. By summer these were being joined by 36-year-olds, and 'many slackers of the Landsturm of the first ban on reprieve'. That autumn, not only was the induction of the 1916 class commenced early, but men 'found deficient before the war' were called to a fresh medical examination. As of

December 1915 'certain specialists' of the 1917 class were called out, and a census taken of the class of 1918. Then, early in 1916, just as the battle of Verdun began to claim the lives of German troops in numbers, the remainder of the class of 1917 was brought into play (US War Office 1917a: 25–31).

Though the German Reservist of 1914 was on average a little older than his counterpart in the Standing Army, there were few other practical differences. Moreover, as new recruits were funnelled into all regiments, the distinction blurred over time. Establishments of Reserve regiments, also organized into three battalions of four companies each, were essentially the same, as were their combat roles, and initial disparities in equipment – as for example in the provision of machine guns and field kitchens – were largely dealt with in the first months of war. Many Reserve divisions attained reputations as good as those of their Standing Army equivalents. Among these were 24. and 26. Reserve-Divisionen, parent formations to Reserve-Infanterie-Regimenter Nr. 104 and Infanterie-Regiment Nr. 180 respectively. American intelligence later described 52. Infanterie-Division, parent to Infanterie-Regiment Nr. 169, as being of 'rather high' morale, still showing 'nerve and dash' a few months after the Somme.

This young soldier of Infanterie-Regiment 'Graf Bose' (1. Thüringisches) Nr. 31 wears a *Pickelhaube* with cover and *Feldgrau* 1910 uniform jacket with a neck cloth. This regiment – one of eight of the Standing Army, plus a further five Reserve regiments, raised in Thuringia – traced its history back to 1812. During World War I it served with 18. Infanterie-Division, facing the French near La Maisonette early in the Somme battle in an area that one German eyewitness recalled as 'just one great field of corpses' (quoted in Sheldon 2005: 237).

# TRAINING, WEAPONS AND TACTICS

## British

Contrary to popular belief, and High Command fears, by mid-1916 the majority of the New Armies' personnel were neither untrained nor inexperienced. In the case of 11th East Lancashire, equipping and drilling in Lancashire was succeeded by more practical training in North Wales and then at Rugeley camp, Staffordshire, including trench digging, mock battle, assault courses and bayonet-fighting. In the summer of 1915 the battalion completed the eight-week musketry course at Ripon. After Yorkshire came Salisbury Plain, from September to December, where the latest kit – in the shape of Lewis guns, hand grenades and signalling equipment – was added to the inventory, and there was more shooting and route marches of up to 15 miles. After this the Pals were shipped out to Egypt before finally, in March 1916, making their way to France, entering a quiet sector in April. Nor was this amount of preparation much out of the ordinary.

Training was topped off by two or three weeks of specific preparation for the 'big push'. While basic tactical evolutions at company and battalion level were governed by 1914's *Infantry Training*, modified in the light of experiences of the sort outlined in *Notes from the Front*, training for the great assault was based on SS109 *Training of Divisions for Offensive Action*, published in May 1916. Five issues were seen as critical: the organization of assembly trenches; bombardment; crossing of the ground between the lines; capture and consolidation of enemy positions including the artillery line; and 'exploitation'.

Manchester Pals dig a machine-gun emplacement in their city's Heaton Park. Manchester raised no fewer than eight Pals battalions; employers supported the drive by releasing men aged 19 to 35, with one month's wages in their pockets and a guarantee of work on return. Men of many occupations joined in large numbers; in 18th (Service) Battalion (3rd City), The Manchester Regiment (or simply 18th Manchester), for example, B Company drew heavily on the personnel of Lloyd's Packing House. The men of 11th East Lancashire experienced this sort of training in North Wales in 1915: trench digging was followed by exercises in which companies took turns to attack and defend the trenches. Any men unable to keep up were sent to Heaton Park for an additional six months of basic training.

A typical brigade attack front was taken to be between 400yd and 600yd. Crucially, *Training of Divisions* ordered that:

> The attack must aim at continuity and must be driven home without intermission, so that the attack gradually works forward till the endurance of the enemy is broken down.
>
> Every attacking unit must be given a limited and clearly defined objective, which it is to capture and consolidate at all costs; the assaulting columns must go right through above ground to this objective in successive waves or lines, each line adding fresh impetus to the preceding line when this is checked, and carrying the whole forward to the objective. The cleaning up and consolidation of positions passed over by the assaulting columns in their advance, the formation of protective flanks, and the preparation of strong supporting points in the captured area will be carried out by other troops of the attacking force, following the assaulting columns and specially told off for the purpose. Local reserves must be held to reinforce those parts of the line which are checked, to fill gaps opening in the front and to relieve troops which are exhausted and whose endurance has gone.
>
> From the moment when the first line of assaulting troops leaves our front trenches, a continuous forward flow must be maintained from the rear throughout the division. (General Staff 1916d)

To maintain momentum, it was further anticipated that when lead units reached their objective, reinforcements might have to be pushed through and over trenches already won. Depth in assaulting columns and marshalling one unit behind another would 'give sufficient driving power to enable the column to reach its objective and to provide sufficient remaining energy to enable the objective to be held when gained'. This was very different from *Infantry Training*, the basic premise of which had been to deploy 'skirmish' lines allowing full use of weapons prior to closing with the enemy. However, *Training of Divisions* admitted much greater flexibility when it came to support weapons, especially: 'The employment of Brigade Machine Gun Companies and Lewis guns, to ensure that full advantage is taken of this great increase in fire power. In particular, opportunities should be looked for to practice pushing forward Lewis guns to precede the attacking infantry or to reinforce an advance which is held up' (General Staff 1916d).

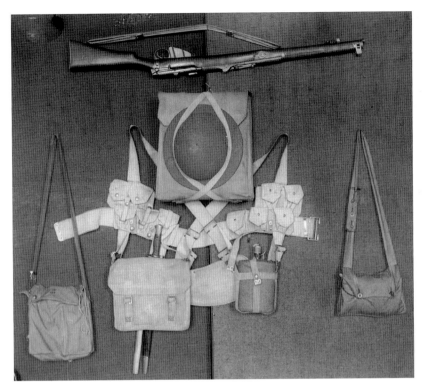

British infantry kit as worn in full 'marching order' by Regulars and Territorials. Immediately under the .303in SMLE rifle is the 1908 Pattern web equipment, with large pack and steel helmet attached. On the waist belt are the small pack or 'haversack', bayonet, entrenching-tool handle and its head in a carrier, and water bottle. The bag to the right is for the 'gas helmet', current during the early stages of the battle; the device worked, but only for limited periods, and as a result two were often carried in the attack. The bag to the left is for the later, much more efficient 'Small Box Respirator'. German gas delivery had diversified to include shells and mortar bombs as well as cylinder release; the largest quantity of German gas used during the battle was diphosgene, or *Perstoff*, which smelled of hay or ripe fruit, and whose containers were marked with a green cross.

Extraordinary as it might now appear, *Training of Divisions* was framed with specific problems in mind. Attacks in the autumn of 1915 were thought to have foundered mainly for two reasons: failure to reinforce swiftly enough, and failure to use sufficient artillery to knock out power of resistance. Lengthy bombardment combined with a mass of infantry continuing to advance according to a pre-planned timetable, irrespective of initial setbacks, appeared to offer the solution. Haig reinforced this analysis when on 15 June he impressed upon his army commanders that:

> The length of each bound forward by the infantry depends on the area which has been prepared by the artillery. The *infantry* must for their part, capture and hold the ground which the artillery has prepared with as little delay as possible … The advance of *isolated detachments* (except for reconnoitring purposes) should be avoided. They lead to the loss of the boldest and the best without result: enemy can concentrate on these detachments. Advance should be uniform. Discipline and the power of subordinate commanders should be exercised to prevent troops getting out of hand. (Haig 2005: 190)

Everything was predicated on the assumption that the artillery would do the killing and clearing and the infantry mop up and move through. However, *Training of Divisions* was already questionable. German assaults at Verdun in February and March followed similar notions, and the Kaiser's commanders had already discovered that where artillery was insufficient, or improperly applied, no amount of infantry in traditional deployments could overcome well-prepared defence in depth supported by automatic weapons. German post-battle analysis took time to percolate to the French, and by the time

This plate shows a corporal in his early 20s as he would have appeared during the assault on Serre on the first day of the Somme battle.

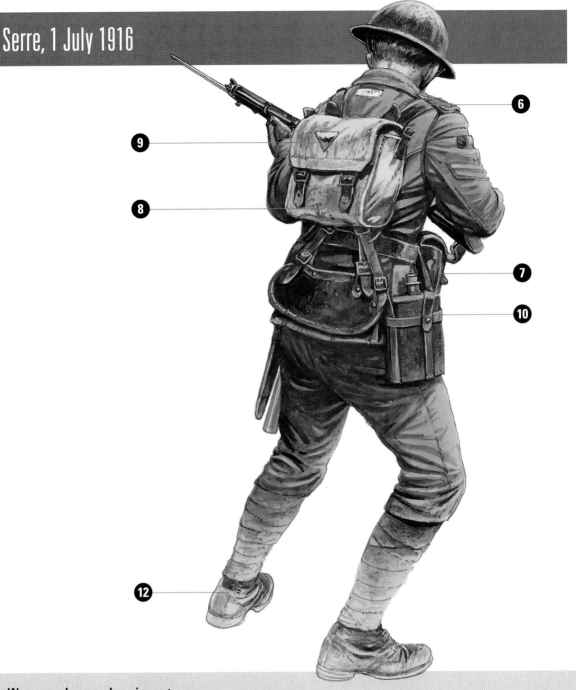

## Weapons, dress and equipment

This 'Pal' is armed with the standard ten-shot .303in Short Magazine Lee Enfield (**1**) with leather sling. Introduced in 1904, the SMLE's short bolt pull and charger-loading magazine gave a rate of fire of over 15 rounds per minute. Designed as a universal weapon for all arms and weighing 8lb 13oz, it was relatively short at 44in, and thus reasonably handy, even in the confines of a trench. His SMLE is fitted with a Pattern 07 sword bayonet with 17in blade (**2**); this particular example has not had the hooked quillon reduced in size.

He wears the steel helmet (**3**) – by July 1916 a standard-issue item – and the four-pocket khaki Service Dress (**4**) with battle patches (**5**) to identify his brigade and battalion. His equipment (**6**) is the leather 1914 type issued to Service battalions; this did its job, but was more susceptible to damp – and never as popular – as the 1908 Pattern web equipment used by Regulars and Territorials. He carries 120 rounds in the waist-belt pouches (**7**), though as with the Germans, extra could be carried in cloth bandoliers. In battle order the small pack (**8**) is worn on the back. According to one source the small metal triangle (**9**) on the pack was cut from biscuit tins; its purpose was to indicate to observers in the rear the progress of British troops. His 2-pint water bottle (**10**) is carried on the right hip, while his gas helmet is carried in a bag (**11**) under his left arm. Brown leather ammunition boots (**12**) are worn.

A star performer of the infantry battle, the .303in Lewis fired from a 47-round drum magazine; it could suffer stoppages, but weighed a comparatively modest 28lb. In 1916 the Germans lacked a similar general-issue weapon, and employed captured Lewis guns and other stopgaps such as the Danish Madsen. *Notes on the Tactical Employment of Machine Guns and Lewis Guns*, issued in March 1916, recommended Lewis guns for giving 'covering fire from the front' during the attack, or pushing out into No Man's Land, into shell holes or other advantageous positions, to harass enemy machine guns and trenches as the infantry went forward.

German *Eierhandgranaten* or 'egg' grenades, first reported during the battle of the Somme, were light enough for a long-range throw, but designed to carry an explosive charge sufficient to clear a single trench bay. New tactics called for egg bombs to be used as part of a bombing team, thrown at targets beyond the range of stick grenades, sometimes over the heads of comrades. Bombs are shown with and without fuses, the example on the left being a practice type.

information could be conveyed to Entente allies, the foundations of *Training of Divisions* were already laid. The overriding strategic necessity was to respond quickly and decisively to events at Verdun – and this both spurred and shaped British actions during that fateful summer and autumn.

## German

German basic training was informed both by the drill regulations of 1906, and by official and unofficial guides, a specified example of which the recruit was often expected to purchase himself. Like British Territorials, German Reservists were expected to undertake a couple of weeks' training each year in peacetime, usually in September. While German training had a reputation for thoroughness, and pre-1914 conscripts spent an entire year preparing for the annual manoeuvres, war brought new problems. The first was the pressure to produce troops more quickly; second, the failure of basic training to keep up with the new realities of combat. Basic training was progressively condensed into three or four months. There was an increasing number of specialist courses, as for example on the machine gun or close-combat weaponry, but although as many men as possible would be put through them, these courses' greatest impact would not be felt until after the Somme. Nevertheless, conscription ensured that a significant portion of the adult male population had pre-war military experience, it being estimated that in 1916 this still extended to over a third of German soldiers.

Infantry training commenced with individual drill and skill at arms, with personal attire, hygiene, marching, saluting and deportment quickly being joined by group weapons training. Though a number of obsolete and captured rifles, and also carbines, saw use during the war, the main infantry arm was the Gewehr 98 Mauser (Gew 98), offering considerable range and accuracy. The penetration of its fully jacketed pointed round was also impressive, being 80cm through wood at 100m (31½in at 109yd), dropping to 40cm at 400m (15¾in at 437yd) and 10cm at 1,800m (4in at 1,969yd). As Major Max von Schreibershofen explained in his *Die Modernen Waffen* of 1914, 'To shoot well, quickly, safely and make great impact on the target: these are the requirements of firearms, and to which the mass of modern weapons correspond'. Nevertheless, it has to be said that while the Mauser was ideal for precision shooting at middle to long range, and its overall length made it useful in

German infantry training began with the individual, working up through sections (*Gruppen*) to training with platoons (*Züge*), companies (*Kompagnien*) and finally battalions (*Bataillone*). Here, troops in training dig a trench traverse. Traverses divided front-line trenches into bays, limiting the effect of shells, and preventing small-arms rounds from passing right along a trench. The tactical solution adopted by the infantry of both sides was to throw grenades over traverses before advancing. Grenade duels were stressful and bloody, but far less costly than frontal attack.

bayonet fighting, its long barrel and bolt pull made it somewhat less handy than the British SMLE for rapid fire or use in confined spaces.

In common with Entente expectations, the assumption of the 1906 drill regulations was that to win the infantry had to attack, and that to attack it had to advance, deploy into linear formation to allow maximum use of weapons, and finally, charge home. The impact of war had modified ideas considerably by mid-1916, with close formations, for example, having been found catastrophic in 1914. New tactics were progressively introduced. On the Somme, those for defence of fixed positions assumed paramount importance. By 1916 there were at least two, and preferably three, 'zones' of trench defence, rather than single trench lines, the advantages offered by crests, forward slopes and long fields of fire being widely and profitably sacrificed for the security of reverse slopes, deeper bunkers and concealment.

In the Somme sector, work on the third position was begun in February 1916, and nearly completed when the battle opened. Unlike the high water-table of Flanders, the Somme region was generally well suited to deep excavations and bunkers. As Sgt Alex Paterson of 11th (Service) Battalion, The Rifle Brigade, explained, 'You went down steps to these places, but the steps didn't go straight down … Ordinary bombs, demolition bombs, would just burst half way down and the worst they would do would be block up the passage, and they always had an escape route … So, first thing, we had to throw down phosphorus bombs – smoke bombs' (quoted in Macdonald 1983: 237–38).

This man's regiment, 9. Rheinisches Infanterie-Regiment Nr. 160, suffered heavily in a hasty counter-attack against the French in the early hours of 4 October: the enemy were closer than predicted and unaffected by bombardment, so managed to pin the Rhinelanders with machine-gun fire. The rifle shown here is the old Mauser Gew 88, 1,245mm (49in) long and weighing 3.8kg (8lb 6oz); many remained in service after the production of the standard-issue Gew 98, also a 7.92mm-calibre weapon with a five-round magazine, but slightly longer and heavier than its predecessor, at 4.09kg (9lb).

This young soldier of Infanterie-Regiment Nr. 169 is depicted as he would have appeared in the struggle for Serre on 1 July 1916.

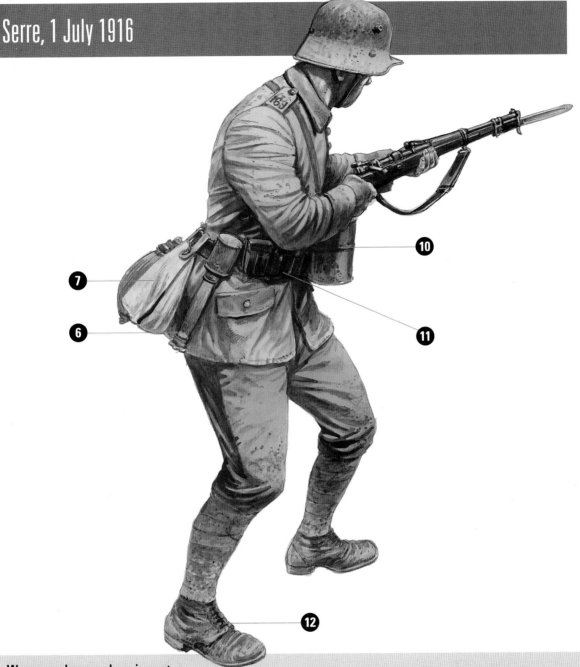

## Weapons, dress and equipment

The Gew 98 Mauser rifle (**1**) carried by this man was one of the most accurate target weapons of the day, well made, and its length was thought to give good 'reach' in bayonet fighting. Nevertheless, its five-round magazine, longer bolt operation and overall length made its rate of fire a little slower than that of the SMLE, and it was not as easy to handle in a confined space as the British weapon. The bayonet (**2**) has a straight edge along the top; a small proportion of German bayonets, usually carried by Pioneers, had a saw-tooth top edge, known as '*mit Säge*'.

This soldier wears the *Feldgrau* uniform (**3**) of 1910, the eight-button jacket featuring flapped side pockets, simplified cuffs and unpiped shoulder-straps. His unit is identified by the regimental number on his shoulder straps (**4**) and red/white/red 2. Kompagnie bayonet knot (**5**). As many of Infanterie-Regiment Nr. 169 fought from their own trenches, most were not required to carry a pack, and, like this man, made do with belt equipment: in this case including a stick grenade (**6**), bread bag (**7**) made of waterproof canvas, water bottle (**8**) and bayonet scabbard (**9**). The 1915-type gas mask, known as the *Gummimaske*, hangs in its steel cylinder (**10**); this often bore the name of the owner in white paint. A total of 120 rounds are carried in 1911-type ammunition pouches (**11**); these were originally issued in natural leather, but were ordered to be blackened in late 1915. He wears ankle boots (**12**) with puttees rather than the marching boots issued to German troops in the early part of the conflict.

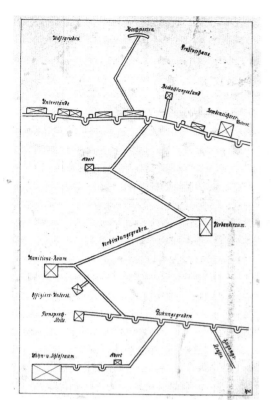

German postcard showing typical elements of the trench system: from top to bottom, it shows a forward sap; front-line fire trenches with dugouts; communication trenches or *Verbindungsgräben*; and cover trench at the rear. There are separate posts for dressing stations; munitions storage; observation; and latrines. Fortified zones and breadth gave 'a certain liberty of action' and allowed best use of the ground, in particular offering the possibility of positioning the main line of defence out of sight, and creating other flanking work, stop lines or strong points. Ideally, front-line trenches were normally manned only by sentries. In the event of attack these were to raise the alarm, drawing others from their shelters. During bombardment the majority of the machine guns were dismounted and taken below, and trench garrisons learned to listen for the slackening of fire ready to take to the defence of the parapet.

In the event of the loss of the trench, local reserves were to make immediate efforts to eject the enemy. One army-level report of September 1915 outlined specifically that in the event of an enemy break-in, it was 'the duty of the neighbouring troops to take him immediately in the flank whether by rifle or machine-gun fire, or by bombing parties from traverse to traverse'. At the same time troops drawn up to the first support line would form 'strong bombing parties' to advance to the aid of those in the front line.

At some point before July 1916, a summary of eight points for defence was issued by XIV. Reserve-Corps for display in front-line dugouts:

1) Our Infantry is superior to any enemy, which it resists courageously or attacks valiantly.

2) Our dugouts resist the heaviest and lengthiest artillery fire, but you need to leave yours in timely fashion and race to the parapet when the enemy attacks. Anyone who remains inside risks death from hand grenades or the effects of gas. So everyone out!

3) Don't store your rifles and hand grenades in the entrances to dugouts, where they can easily become buried. Take them with you into the dugout! The same applies to machine guns.

4) Don't be afraid of gas attacks – even if they darken the sky. The gas will pass over to the rear quickly. Put on your protective equipment and light fires of old wooden boxes in front of you! Only troops who have lost their heads during a gas attack have been thrown back by the enemy; those who have stood firm have beaten back attacks.

5) Use your rifle initially from the parapet! Only throw grenades when the enemy has closed right up. They are often thrown too soon.

6) If the enemy has broken into the trench, continue the fight with hand grenades! Help will arrive immediately from the flanks and rear and everyone must go to the aid of their neighbours if the enemy breaks in there.

7) If there is an enemy breakthrough, don't lose your head! Only feeble troops surrender. Brave troops conduct a fighting withdrawal. In this way courageous companies have taken thousands of prisoners in recent battles.

8) Soldiers will always be re-supplied with food and drink, even if the battle lasts for days. (Quoted in Sheldon 2005: 83)

# LEADERSHIP

## British

Initially, commanding officers of New Army battalions forwarded the names of potential officers to the War Office for approval. The majority of these men had been educated in a public or grammar school; most were well motivated, and many were not complete novices as a substantial proportion had received basic training through the Officer Training Corps, or the Territorials.

Nevertheless, some were commissioned merely on the strength of holding responsible positions in civilian life. Remarkably, some New Army battalions – for example, 15th (Service) Battalion (1st Leeds), The Prince of Wales's Own (West Yorkshire Regiment) – were found to hold significant pools of potential officer material, and many rankers were later commissioned. One Territorial battalion – 1/28th (County of London) Battalion (Artist's Rifles), The London Regiment – was converted to officer training early in 1916, eventually producing more than 10,000 new officers. Infantry-officer casualties were particularly high, however, and by 1916 it had become customary to 'leave out of battle' a portion of both officers and men, usually including the battalion second-in-command, around whom it would be possible to rebuild the unit in event of disaster.

VC-winner 2/Lt T. Adlam of 7th Bedfordshire recalled his relationship with his men: 'I had a very happy platoon. Perhaps that's because I'm a good mixer. And, always, if anyone could do something better than me, I let them do it. Some officers would think they had to do better than their men. But if I found a man who could do something better than me I'd say, "Well, you do that." And I think they liked it' (quoted in Levine 2008: 60–61). (© Imperial War Museum (Q 69155))

Some of the 'committee men', who had been essentially self-appointed leaders early in the history of the Pals, did stand aside when their battalions were accepted by the state, but it made little difference given universal shortage of infantry-officer talent, occasioned both by the small size of the Army in 1914 and early losses. Lt-Col R. Sharples, who had retired from the local Territorials in 1911 aged 60 and was appointed 11th East Lancashire's first commanding officer, was soon succeeded by Lt-Col A.W. Rickman, a Regular who was enthusiastically welcomed by his men, as Pte George Pollard recalled: 'He was very smart, a true professional … We were looking at a real soldier for the first time. We knew he would sort us out' (quoted in Holmes 2005: 84). Rickman insisted upon adherence to King's Regulations, telling two officers who shaved off their moustaches to 'Get off my parade and don't come back until they're grown again' (quoted in Holmes 2005: 366).

Perhaps the most obvious difference between the New Armies and their enemies was that few New Army officers had extensive battle experience in mid-1916. This may have made them more anxious to demonstrate dependability, and to operate 'by the book' strictly in accordance with the minutiae of orders. Interestingly, German sources also concluded that discipline was actually stricter in the Kitchener New Army battalions, and the bearing of individuals 'more rigid', than in the Regulars (Duffy 2006: 70).

Cpl Harry Aspinall, 11th East Lancashire, of Rishton, Lancashire, pictured in October 1916. Aspinall fought on the first day of the Somme, but was killed, aged 24, in February 1918. Chosen from the more experienced, or men showing aptitude, lance corporals and corporals directed their sections, or relayed orders from senior NCOs and platoon commanders. As of August 1914 it was hoped that NCOs for new formations could be found from re-enlisted Regular NCOs, and men 'promoted from the rank they formerly held'; lance corporals were to be selected from old soldiers and suitable new recruits. 11th East Lancashire's initial RSM was an old soldier of 60 who had fought the Native Americans in the United States, the Zulu and the Boers. In practice there were never enough competent old soldiers still fit enough to do the job, and many New Army NCOs soon had to be found from the ranks.

The strong emphasis upon planning and scheduling the attack in *Training of Divisions* severely – and deliberately – sought to constrain local commanders' independence of action. In order that nothing be left to chance, it was observed that 'it must be remembered that officers and troops generally do not now possess that military knowledge arising from a long and high state of training which enables them to act promptly on sound lines in unexpected situations. They have become accustomed to deliberate action based on precise and detailed orders' (General Staff 1916d). This would lead to prescriptions that many brigade and battalion commanders would not feel able to countermand. It is tempting to deduce that it was both the strict discipline and the inexperience of some officers of New Army formations that led them to stick religiously to the letter of *Training of Divisions* when others ignored detail when it seemed appropriate to do so, shaping action to circumstance.

## German

Arguably, the pre-war German officer corps was even more selective than the British, and widely regarded as a bastion of political conservatism. Nobility and, more recently, wealth were passports to command. Nevertheless, the war and the resultant dire shortage of officers would perforce draw out not only a mass of socially less well-qualified Reservists, but also force the pace in terms of creating *Offizierstellvertreter*, 'substitute' officers with commissions valid only for the duration of the war. These approximated to the British 'temporary' commissions.

German officer training was demanding, often requiring levels of responsibility to be assumed well above nominal rank – an idea actively encouraged by Generalfeldmarschall Alfred Graf von Schlieffen (1833–1913), the original architect of the German plan to defeat France that bore his name. Conversely, it increasingly became expected that officers should be capable of responding proactively to direction, fulfilling its spirit with initiative rather than waiting for prescriptive orders. As of 1916 line-infantry units were accustomed to drawing together specialist teams for attack or counter-attack. So it was, for example, that the order of battle of 24. Reserve-Division, current on 14 July 1916, listed a *Sächsisches Sturm Kompanie (Abkommandierte aus der Truppe)* – a Saxon assault company 'commanded from the troops', in this instance Reserve-Infanterie-Regimenter Nrs. 104, 107 and 133. Such teams were trained in new assault techniques, but were not part of the army-level 'storm battalions'.

The latest innovations in warfare were exhibited to infantry officers to keep them abreast of developments, as Reserve-Leutnant Kimmich of II. Bataillon/Infanterie-Regiment Nr. 180 recalled:

'In the trenches': an artist's impression of a German trench garrison, probably in late 1915. The trench follows an old tree line and is loop-holed to the front and provided with cubby-holes for munitions. The officer, foreground, is preparing a rifle grenade for launching. In some cases the men who commanded the German regiments garrisoning the Somme had not only familiarized themselves with the terrain – they had actually shaped it. Upon arriving in the Somme sector in April 1916, Reserve-Infanterie-Regiment Nr. 99's Major von Fabeck had designed a major defensive work in the Saint-Pierre Divion sector, and gave his name to the Fabeck-Graben that would be the scene of so much fighting in the Somme battle (Duffy 2006: 150).

Mit Genehmigung der Illustrirten Zeitung, Leipzig.

Im Schützengraben.

In the morning we drive in the staff coach of the 1st Bn 180 to Biefvillers [near Bapaume] to the flammenwerfer [flamethrower] demonstration. What extraordinary means are adopted to send men from life to death. A stream of burning oil sets the entire garrison of a trench on fire. The smoke has a great moral effect. It is very suitable to clear up an English nest [improvised defensive position]. (Quoted in Barton 2006: 162)

While staff work and officers played the most important roles in both strategy and the organization of training, most practical aspects were taught to other ranks by NCOs. Privately produced manuals were also aimed at NCOs and officers. One of these was *Lehnerts Handbuch für den Truppenführer*, updated by Major Friedrich Immanuel in 1912. Before the war about a quarter of German NCOs were educated from their teenage years in special training schools. Others were picked out as promising during conscript service and offered the opportunity to re-enlist. A significant incentive was that after 12 years' service, an NCO with a good record was guaranteed a civil-service position.

# MORALE, MOTIVATION AND LOGISTICS

## British

Many New Army men were well satisfied with what had been achieved in training: one soldier of The York and Lancaster Regiment writing for the *Barnsley Chronicle* from Salisbury Plain was certainly upbeat about what he saw as the successful transition from a crowd of colliers to 'a New Army of fighting men, trained and skilled in the new and latest devices of modern war'.

The soldiers of Britain's New Armies often had an ambivalent attitude to their enemy. 2/Lt Adlam of 7th Bedfordshire recalled the response of one of his men when confronted with the enemy at close quarters during the attack on the Schwaben Redoubt:

There was a German soldier just at the dugout. He'd been wounded. He was in a bad way. He was just moaning 'Mercy kamerad! Mercy kamerad!' And this fellow in front of me – one of the nicest fellows I had in my platoon – said, 'Mercy, you bloody German? Take that!' And he pointed point-blank at him. But he jerked, and missed him. And I gave him a shove from behind, and I said, 'Go on! He won't do any harm. Let's go and get a good one!' But it was so funny, the fellow said afterwards, 'Sir, glad I missed him, Sir.' It was just in the heat of the moment, you see. (Quoted in Levine 2008: 237)

Although the transit of supplies to the front line often broke down under the strains imposed

Lt-Gen Sir Aylmer Hunter-Weston, GOC VIII Corps, right, with French politician Georges Clemenceau. Pte James Snailham of 11th East Lancashire later recalled hearing a pep-talk from Lt-Gen Hunter-Weston on 29 June in which the men were encouraged to 'do their bit cheerily in the big push' while the artillery so destroyed the enemy trenches and wire that 'not even a rat' would survive. Hunter-Weston's command fared particularly badly on 1 July, a fact attributed in part to his decision to explode the mine at Hawthorn Ridge ten minutes early.

Capable of throwing a 114kg (251lb) shell over 9,000m (9,850yd), the 21cm Mörser was one of the more effective German bunker-busting pieces faced by the British on the Somme. A crucial element of British training was getting acquainted with artillery, as Pte George Pollard of 11th East Lancashire recalled: 'Then I heard a noise. I first thought of a train coming, but it was a train coming through the air and blowing up around me. A shell crashed only yards away. I was never so scared in my life. I tried to get in a small dug out but it was already full of men (the old hands knew what was coming). I got down on my knees at the bottom of the trench with the other men. I thanked God I had a spade to put over my head ...' (quoted in Turner 1993: 123).

by frequent bombardment and poor communications, and growing young men always wanted more, the British soldier was usually better fed than his enemy. Significantly, some acute equipment shortages experienced early in the war had now been addressed. The combat load carried on the offensive varied considerably, but usually depended upon the wave of the attack to which a soldier was committed. The first or 'assault' wave was usually the most lightly equipped. So it was that instructions to the Salford Pals of 15th (Service) Battalion (1st Salford), The Lancashire Fusiliers outlined the following for 1 July:

A) Fighting kit will be worn. The mess tin to be inside the haversack, and to contain pack of iron rations. Steel helmet; water bottle filled; 2 bandoliers of SAA [Small Arms Ammunition – 100 rounds] in addition to the 120 rounds carried in pouches; 2 sand bags under flap of haversack; unexpended portion of days rations; 1 iron ration; 1 tin of meat and four biscuits.

B) Two gas helmets will be worn, one attached to the shirt as already demonstrated, the other slung over the left shoulder in the usual manner. The satchel for the gas helmet attached to the shirt will be placed in the haversack. The top three buttons of the tunic will be left undone so as to facilitate the adjustment of helmets …

D) Each officer, NCO, and man will carry 2 bombs in his pockets. Except in the case of bombers, these will not be used by the carrier but will be dumped under platoon arrangements, when the final position has been taken up, from this dump bombers will replenish their supplies.

The munition worker's contribution to 'the big push'. With the help of female labour, British production increased massively so that in the month of June 1916 alone 3.7 million artillery shells were made, rising to 4.5 million in July, and 5.4 million in August. Annual rifle production accelerated from 120,000 in 1914 to 1,300,000 in 1916, while the 266 Vickers guns produced in the second half of 1914 were dwarfed by the 7,400 made in 1916; there were only eight Lewis guns made in the UK in 1914, but 21,600 produced in 1916.

THE BIG PUSH

Munition Worker: "Well, I'm not taking a holiday myself just yet, but I'm sending these kids of mine for a little trip on the Continent."

This loading approximates to a little over 60lb, much the same as that carried by British troops in World War II. 'Bombing parties', such as those attached to 11th East Lancashire, omitted some of the ammunition but attracted other burdens, the eight men of each team being encumbered with 100 Mills bombs, and 25 rifle grenades and their attendant cartridges and detonators. They also carried eight canvas 'bomb buckets', including two intended to replenish the supply of bombs from men carrying the reserve supplies.

However, in subsequent waves, those not actually intended to fight but for reinforcement and consolidation, burdens were increased very significantly by a mass of impedimenta including picks, shovels, axes, more sand bags, signals equipment, extra munitions, barbed wire, and the like. In such instances loads exceeding 100lb were possible, and could prove catastrophic under fire.

On a man-for-man basis it is arguable that the 'Pals' had a slight advantage over a heavily shelled and less-well-provisioned enemy. In practice, counter-bombardment, machine guns, less experienced officers and the tactical demand to cross open ground threw an overwhelming advantage to the defenders.

## German

Initially, German morale in the Somme sector was good. Unteroffizier Otto Lais of Infanterie-Regiment Nr. 169 recalled the morale-boosting role performed by his divisional commander, Generalleutnant Karl von Borries:

> Our divisional commander, our beloved 'little Excellency' (he is of small stature) often made daily inspections, coming in all weathers and at 'worse' times! Usually unaccompanied, wearing a shabby windcheater, he went along the trenches, climbed down into the dugouts, clambered over the spoil, squeezed at night through the lanes of barbed wire, was here, was there, was everywhere. He had a particular liking for his machine-gunners and it always gave us special pleasure when we were allowed to show and demonstrate our spick-and-span weapon to him. Generalleutnant von Borries never made a big deal of himself or of the performance of his division, just as his favourite Regiment 169 never made a fuss of itself and its successes. (Lais 1935)

As the fighting wore on, however, the reinforcements sent to the front did not compare favourably to those who had fallen in battle, as Württemberger Georg Bucher recalled:

> The drafts displayed a sense of regimental honour as keen as that of the experienced 'front hogs': their arms drill was a joy to see; their shooting was, on the whole, up to the normal standard; and their discipline was entirely excellent. But, and unfortunately, they had … little notion of trench warfare … the rest could be accompanied in the field – there were infantry depots behind the front designed precisely for that purpose; unfortunately it wasn't possible to put every draft through their mill. (Bucher 2006: 90)

The general German impression was that their adversary was well equipped, fed and motivated. Many Germans appear to have been well disposed towards individual British soldiers they encountered.

'The front-line soldier' – from a postcard sent home to Germany in late 1916. No pack is carried but many items have been stuffed into bags and pockets. Additions to the bedraggled uniform include an ammunition bandolier, woollen scarf and 'headover', and a cloth gas-mask bag. Codenamed 'White Star', the main gas used by the British on the Somme was a mixture of phosgene and chlorine. German gas defence was arguably more advanced than British in July 1916, with infantry using improved versions of the 1915 rubberized fabric *Gummimaske*. Though these were previously carried in cloth bags, from April 1916 a protective steel cylinder was issued. The mask had eye-pieces and screw-fit filter that could be changed: the latest filters incorporated three layers, combining *Diatomit* granules, charcoal, potash and hexamine.

Overloading soldiers was already the subject of black humour even in 1916. In fact, although 'carrying' or 'working parties' were often called upon to shift rations, ammunition and building materials, the equipment in which the soldier usually 'stood to' in defence of his position was perhaps 50lb, being the standard 61lb as outlined in the *Field Service Pocket Book*, minus the greatcoat, cap, large pack and some small items, but plus steel helmet and gas helmet. At least 18lb of the load carried by the soldier of a trench garrison was accounted for by rifle and ammunition.

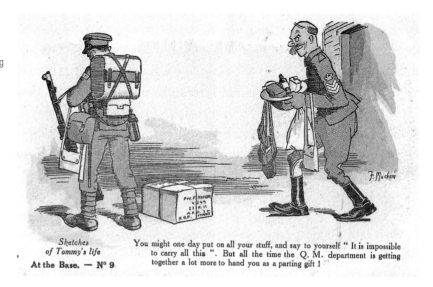

*Sketches of Tommy's life*
**At the Base. — Nº 9**

You might one day put on all your stuff, and say to yourself " It is impossible to carry all this ". But all the time the Q. M. department is getting together a lot more to hand you as a parting gift ! "

For example, Feldwebel Karl Stumpf of Infanterie-Regiment Nr. 169, garrisoning Serre, recalled: 'Before the bombardment started and while everything was peaceful, I could see through my periscope a young Englishman playing his trumpet every evening. We used to wait for this hour but suddenly there was nothing to be heard and we all hoped that nothing had happened to him' (quoted in Middlebrook 1984: 59).

German provision of essential supplies became increasingly more questionable under Allied blockade. Like their enemies, the Germans accumulated equipment with the passage of time. Though carrying large quantities of kit was as detrimental to the German soldier as it was to his enemy, during defensive battle – and with the obvious exception of water and munitions – much could be left where it lay.

British prisoners, including, centre, a smoking Lancashire Fusilier wearing 1914 winter cap and 'LF' brass shoulder titles. Oberstleutnant Alfons Bram – commander of Königlich Bayerische 8. Reserve-Infanterie-Regiment, which was caught up in the fighting at the Schwaben Redoubt on 1 July – was impressed by the British performance on the Somme: 'It can be seen that the British have succeeded in taking their young soldiers, who physically are almost all young powerful men, the great majority of whom are drawn from the working class (clear from examination of their paybooks!) and turning them into effective fighters. British morale was good … The standard of training is good. Very specific drills for attack and defence appear to have been practised during training' (quoted in Sheldon 2005: 225–28).

# Serre

## 1 July 1916

## BACKGROUND TO BATTLE

At the northern end of the main attack front, 31st (New Army) Division was handed one of the most difficult tasks of 1 July: to advance up a slope from a row of small copses on ground retaken by the French in 1915, in order to seize the village of Serre, held by Major von Struensee's 8. Badisches Infanterie-Regiment Nr. 169. Other assets nearby included Major Julius von Stoeklern zu Grünholzek's 3. Magdeburgisches Infanterie-Regiment Nr. 66, also of 52. Infanterie-Division, to the north, and *in extremis* any elements of Oberst Josenhanss's Württembergers of Reserve-Infanterie Regiment Nr. 121 (26. Reserve-Division) that were not engaged, to the south.

Leading 31st Division's advance on 1 July, 94th Brigade had a plan of attack that appeared relatively straightforward. The evening before the offensive, the Pals would march 6 miles to the front, threading their way through to the departure trenches. At 0720hrs, under cover of the barrage, the first wave would leave their trenches, bayonets fixed, and advance, 'in extended order as near the German front line as our barrage permitted, and lay down' (TNA WO 95/2363). At 0725hrs

A German communication trench through a ruined village; the sign indicates right, for the company commander's post, office and kitchen, and left to the platoon commander, 1st Platoon. Note how narrow this particular trench is, and how this would have hampered the progress of heavily laden soldiers. At Serre on 1 July 1916, four of Infanterie-Regiment Nr. 169's 12 rifle companies – 4., 3., 6. and 7. – occupied the front line, while 1., 2., 8. and 5. manned the second and third lines; 9., 10. and 11. held the trenches defending the village, while 12. Kompagnie acted as reserve, in and behind Serre itself.

The attacking British faced an awesome task, as depicted in this French diagram illustrating the extreme difficulty of assaulting field fortifications. Attacking troops outnumbering defenders 12 to one are whittled away to parity over an 800m (875yd) advance. Where defenders have machine guns, a force 14 times stronger is shattered even if fire is withheld to the last 300m (328yd).

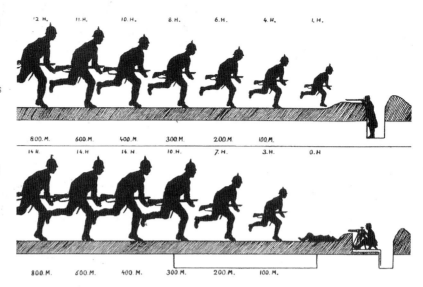

the second wave would advance and lie down 50yd behind the first. At 0730hrs the barrage would lift from the German front line, and move on to more distant targets; all four waves would now advance simultaneously as the third and fourth left their trenches.

In the attack Lt-Col A.W. Rickman's 11th East Lancashire deployed 720 men, on a frontage of about 350yd. In the first wave, under Capt A.B. Tough, would go two platoons each of W and X companies; in the second under Capt H. Livesey, were the remaining two platoons of W and X. The third wave, under Lt G.G. Williams, was similarly comprised of two platoons each from Y and Z companies, and finally the fourth wave, under Capt H.D. Riley, was made up of the remaining two platoons of Y and Z companies. The first British objective was the enemy trenches opposite; the second, the village of Serre; and the third, a point north-east of the village, where the battalion would form part of a defensive line to protect the northern flank of the entire Somme offensive. From the first whistle to occupying the final position, the action was intended to take 110 minutes.

Nearly all the British battalions attacking that morning assaulted the Germans head on, but to the obvious perils of frontal attack against a prepared position was added the danger of flanking fire. High Command was not blind to this issue, which was a major reason for the diversionary attack on Gommecourt, about 2½ miles to the north. Here, 46th and 56th Divisions were supposed to take and clear what was potentially a dangerous thorn in the side of the main assault, calling onto themselves fire that might otherwise fall on the flank of 31st Division. The men of 46th and 56th divisions certainly attracted fire, at least initially, and suffered 5,000 casualties, but did not divert any German troops away from the main zone of attack, and as the diversion at Gommecourt withered, German guns could be trained freely to any direction under threat.

Infanterie-Regiment Nr. 169 had endured a mind-numbing week leading up to the attack, suffering approximately 200 casualties from a total strength of about 2,400. The worst of the shelling came in the concluding minutes of the final morning, as the British guns were joined by a 'hurricane

bombardment' from trench mortars. As the war diary of the regiment recorded,

> Early on the 24th June, the preliminary artillery bombardment began, at first with light calibres, then progressively going over to medium and heavy calibres, as well as the heaviest mortar shells over the first four lines of trenches. Many dugouts were destroyed. Supplies of food and munitions were possible only through the most determined efforts of the supply troops. Nightly trench raids by English companies during the later nights were repulsed. Early on the 1st July, patrols of the 4th 169 and 7th 169 observed and reported the manning of the enemy forward positions. In a state of great expectation, all parts of the regiment were prepared for the sight of the enemy onslaught. (Jackson 1924)

## INTO COMBAT

Given the final crescendo of the British barrage, what followed was expected by the German defenders – and even a relief: 'Over there in closed rifle ranks, come the attacking English. Slowly, almost leisurely, they trot along, out of the third into the second, then into the first English trench. From there they proceed to the attack, their light "cooking utensils" flash in the gunpowder impregnated air.' Otto Lais continues:

> 'They're coming'. The sentries, who had to remain outside throughout the drumfire, rise out of the shell-holes. Dust and dirt lie a centimetre-thick on their faces and uniforms. Their cry of warning rings piercingly in the narrow gaps that form the dugout entrance. 'Get out ... get out ... they're coming!' Now men rush to the surface and throw themselves into shell holes and craters; now they fling themselves in readiness at the crater's rim; now they rush forward under cover from the former second and third lines and place themselves in the first line of defence. Hand-grenades are being hauled by the box from shell-hole to shell-hole. (Lais 1935)

Brig-Gen H.C. Rees was eyewitness to the attack of his own 94th Brigade: 'The attack began at 7.30am, but ten minutes before zero our guns opened an intense fire. I stood on top to watch. It was magnificent. The trenches in front of Serre changed shape and dissolved minute by minute under the terrific hail of steel. Watching, I began to believe in the possibility of a great success, but I reckoned without the Hun artillery' (IWM: Doc 77/179/1). Lais continues: 'We call for a barrage! Red flares climb high then fade away as they fall to the ground. Destructive fire and barrage fire leave masses of green and red marks in the sky! Dear God! The German barrage fire!' (Lais 1935). Rees goes on:

An original tattered annotated print from the East Lancashire Regiment collection showing Serre, right, from the air prior to the attack of 1 July. Zigzagging communication trenches radiate from the already ruined village, cutting through the fire trenches, which run predominantly north to south. The solid German positions at Serre on 1 July 1916 were described by Unteroffizier Otto Lais of Infanterie-Regiment Nr. 169: 'The second, the third, the fourth trench get deeper and deeper dugouts. Thirty, forty and fifty steps go deep down. Hewed tree-trunks, beams and T-bars, sacks of angle irons and scaffolding clamps are hauled from the supply depots. The entrances to the shelters, and dugout recesses are strengthened and reinforced. Even some of the approach trenches, the L3, the L5 and the notorious and feared L6 get dugouts and depots in their backward areas' (Lais 1935). (Duke of Lancaster's Regiment)

## MAP KEY

**1** **0240hrs:** Having set off at 1900hrs the previous evening, Lt-Col Rickman's 11th East Lancashire reaches the damaged assembly trenches. About 20 minutes later, Rickman commences the retirement of his battalion to the second trench line.

**2** **0720hrs:** The Hawthorn Ridge mine detonates to the south, and the British mount a trench-mortar 'hurricane' barrage; following 65 minutes of more intensive shelling from the British artillery, the British bombardment lifts beyond the first-line German trenches. The men of 11th East Lancashire fix bayonets, and the first wave advances into No Man's Land and goes prone. Two minutes later, the second wave of 11th East Lancashire enters the front-line trench, and then at 0725hrs advances to lie down 50yd behind the first, as the Germans begin to emerge from bunkers and are observed in their front-line trenches.

**3** **0730hrs:** 'Zero hour': the British third and fourth waves leave Campion and Monk trenches and begin to move forward within the British position as the British barrage moves to German fourth line. The German barrage falls on No Man's Land and the British front line. The British first wave stands

and advances into No Man's Land, followed two minutes later by the second wave, and then the third and fourth waves. At 0739hrs Rickman reports the advance of the first two waves 'according to time table' – but they have already suffered heavy casualties.

**4** **0755hrs:** Five minutes after Rickman reports that all four waves are advancing – but begins to realize that the attack is probably a failure – 94th Brigade receives reports that the German front line has been seized and British troops have reached the German second line, and begins attempts at reinforcement. At 0835hrs the German artillery is redirected onto the Germans' own front line, and soon falls upon British reinforcements.

**5** **1015hrs:** The British third and fourth waves are still engaged in German positions. Returning British wounded report that the enemy front line is still held by the Germans, and 94th Brigade receives intelligence of German 'bombing parties' working their way forward along communication trenches. Fighting is observed as far back as Serre. By 1200hrs, however, with reports of failure and wounded still returning, the British front line is reorganized for defence.

## Battlefield environment

Despite a week of shelling of the enemy trenches, vegetation remained on the ground around the British position. Light rain during the night and the thin morning mist noted by British artillery observers cleared by zero hour on 1 July. In the hollow below Serre, among and behind the four 'Apostles' copses, assembly trenches offered welcome cover for 31st Division. However, on the other side of the line a majority of Infanterie-Regiment Nr. 169's personnel survived in deep bunkers, and much of the wire was uncut. In the S2 sector

a slight fold in the terrain, mentioned in the Badeners' war diary, offered a slim opportunity for 11th East Lancashire to close with the enemy before catastrophic loss intervened. With the Pals ascending a slope, much would depend on how quickly the Germans could train their artillery and man their front-line trenches after the British barrage lifted.

A view from the centre right of Serre village today, looking across No Man's Land towards the British lines. (Martin Pegler)

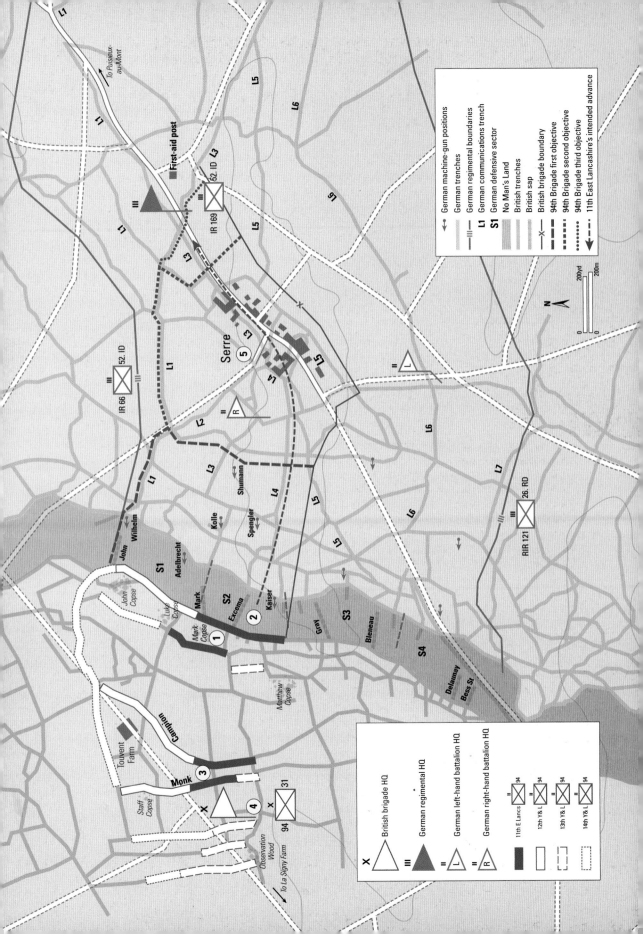

To Puisieux-au-Mont

First-aid post

52. ID  L3

IR 169

III  52. ID

IR 66

L5

L5

L6

L6

L7

Serre

⑤

L1

L2

L3

Kolle

Shumann

Spengler

L4

L5

L6

L7

26. RD

RIR 121

John

Wilhelm

Adelbrecht

S1

Mark

Excema

S2

②

Kaiser

Grey

S3

Bieneau

S4

Delaunay

Bess St

John Copse

Luke Copse

Mark Copse

①

Matthew Copse

Campion

Touvent Farm

Monk

③

Staff Copse

④

94

31

Observation Wood

To La Signy Farm

N

L =

R =

**Legend (top right):**

- German machine-gun positions
- German trenches
- German regimental boundaries
- German communications trench
- *L1* German defensive sector
- *S1* German defensive sector
- No Man's Land
- British trenches
- British sap
- —X— British brigade boundary
- 94th Brigade first objective
- 94th Brigade second objective
- 94th Brigade third objective
- 11th East Lancashire's intended advance

200yd

200m

**Legend (bottom):**

- X  British brigade HQ
- ▲  German regimental HQ
- =L  German left-hand battalion HQ
- =R  German right-hand battalion HQ

- 11th E Lancs  =  94
- 12th Y&L  =  94
- 13th Y&L  =  94
- 14th Y&L  =  94

This ten minutes intense bombardment combined with the explosion of twenty tons of dynamite under the Hawthorn Redoubt near Beaumont Hamel must have convinced any enemy observer that the attack was in progress and, as our infantry advanced, down came a perfect wall of explosive along the front trenches of my Brigade and the 93rd [to the south]. It was the most frightful artillery display that I had seen up to that time and in some ways I think it was the heaviest barrage I have seen put down by the defence on any occasion. (IWM: Doc 77/179/1)

The possible need for defensive positions, at least on limited sectors, had been anticipated by the Germans well before the outbreak of war, and instructions on field works had been issued as an all-arms manual in 1911. Here a 7.92mm MG 08 machine gun, protected with an armoured barrel jacket, is emplaced in an earth-and-log bunker; the crew are equipped with 1915-type 'ball' grenades for close defence. The sledge mount incorporated small boxes for stowage of spare parts and tools. Fed from cloth belts, the water-cooled MG 08 had a cyclic rate of up to 500 rounds per minute and weighed 48lb; the sledge mount added a further 75lb.

One company officer of 11th East Lancashire described the German counter-bombardment as 'one of the most consistently severe I had seen. When it fell it gave the impression of a thick belt of poplar trees from the cones of the explosions. As soon as I saw it I ordered every man within reach to halt or lie down. It was impossible for any but a few men to get through it' (quoted in Barton 2006: 84).

Musketier Karl Blenk of Infanterie-Regiment Nr. 169 recalled his impressions of the opening stages of the attack:

When the English started advancing we were very worried; they looked as though they must overrun our trenches. We were very surprised to see them walking, we had never seen that before. I could see them everywhere; there were hundreds. The officers were in front. I noticed one of them walking calmly, carrying a walking stick … If only they had run, they would have overwhelmed us. (Quoted in Middlebrook 1984: 157)

Rees went on:

At the time this barrage really became intense … I have never seen a finer display of individual and collective bravery than the advance of that brigade. I never saw a man waver from the exact line prescribed for him. Each line disappeared in the thick cloud of dust and smoke which rapidly blotted out the whole area … I saw a few groups of men through gaps in the smoke cloud, but I knew that no troops could hope to get through such a fire. (IWM: Doc 77/179/1)

Pte James Snailham was hit by artillery fire: 'I went over the top at 0730 and my next-door pal was killed straight away. I kept going and going, being the youngest [Snailham had turned 18 that March], and daftest I suppose. I got as far as the Jerry wire, before a shell exploded and a lump went through my leg. I laid there until seven o'clock in the evening' (quoted in Levine 2008: 110). The first two waves hit the German trenches depleted and intermixed – the second wave now accelerating out of the barrage to catch up. Pte C. Glover, orderly to Capt Livesey, was in the thick of it:

Five Germans came from nowhere, the first of whom hurled a bomb which grazed Captain Livesey's face but didn't explode. Captain Livesey shot at the group with his revolver. More Germans came up so Captain Livesey and I made for a shell hole just as a shell landed nearby. I must have been knocked out. When I came round I looked for Captain Livesey but couldn't find him. At length I gave him up as lost. I was wounded … My cigarette case had turned a bullet which made a slight wound in my side and my gas helmet had stopped another from doing much damage. I was also wounded in the thumb. (Quoted in Turner 1993: 146)

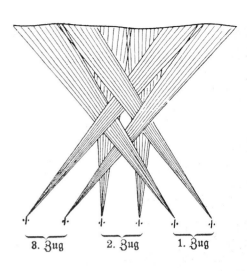

Though the German barrage had inflicted much initial damage, machine guns were now chopping holes through the ranks of the remainder of the attacking British infantry:

A German manual illustration showing how the three platoons of a machine-gun company may be deployed to produce interlocking zones of fire. Note how the cones of fire become wider, but more diffused, at longer ranges. Although the MG 08 was not known for its mobility, according to Brig-Gen Rees, the Germans at Serre 'actually ran a machine gun out into No Man's Land to help repel the attack' (IWM: Doc 77/179/1).

Amidst all the roar, the clatter, the rumble and the bursts, the lashing out and wild firing of the riflemen, the firm, regular beat of our machine-guns is solid and calm; – tack-tack-tack-tack … this one slower, the other faster in rhythm! – precision work in materials and construction! – a terrible melody to the enemy, it gives a greater degree of security and inner calm to our own friends in the infantry and to the other ranks …

One belt after another is raced through! 250 shots – 1,000 shots – 3,000 shots. 'Bring up the spare gun-barrels!' shouts the gun commander. The gun barrel's changed – carry on shooting! – 5,000 shots – the gun-barrel has to be changed again. The barrel's scorching hot, the coolant's boiling – the gunners' hands are nearly scorched, scalded. 'Carry on shooting,' urges the gun commander, 'or be shot yourself!' The coolant in the gun jacket boils, vaporized by the furious shooting. In the heat of battle, the steam hose comes away from the opening of the water can into which the steam's meant to re-condense. A tall jet of steam sprays upwards, a fine target for the enemy. It's lucky for us that the sun's shining in their eyes and that it's behind us. (Lais 1935)

From the point of view of 11th East Lancashire, things looked very different, as Pte Will Marshall – in the fourth wave – later recalled:

We were sitting ducks … They were sweeping across, and lots of men were falling at either side … My section there was only three of us left, well there wasn't another man for 60 yards either side … another shell came and I were blown off my feet onto the floor – didn't know where I were for a minute and when I picked myself up these two were missing and there was only me there. A bit of shrapnel had hit me in the arm and another across me leg … I came back and there was just as much danger as coming forward. (NWSA)

What appeared incredible was that even after the British ranks were blown to shreds and intensively machine-gunned, surviving Pals crossed the German front lines of the first objective, and continued with the plan. L/Cpl H. Bury, one of 11th East Lancashire's signallers who had been held back from the attack in order to follow when the enemy trenches had been captured, could see the unfolding action: 'We were able to see our comrades move forward in

## Will Marshall, 11th East Lancashire

L/Cpl 15369 W. Marshall, a weaver at the Parks Head mill, volunteered in September 1914 aged 21 with the blessing of his parents. Not long after swearing his oath 'to serve his Majesty the King' at Burnley barracks he exchanged civilian clothes for a uniform of 'Melton Blue' accompanied by kit bag, boots, various sundries and non-functioning 'drill' rifle. By July 1916 he had been trained and re-equipped for the 'Big Push'. 'I saw many men fall back into the trench as they attempted to climb out. Those of us who managed had to walk two yards apart … We all had to keep in line. Machine gun bullets were sweeping backwards and forwards and hitting the ground around our feet. Shells were bursting everywhere. I had no special feeling of fear except I knew we must all go forward until wounded or killed. There was no going back' (NWSA). Despite his wounds Marshall lived a long and active life, and died in 1995.

an attempt to cross No Man's Land, only to be mown down like meadow grass. I felt sick at the sight of this carnage and remember weeping. We did actually see a flag signalling near the village of Serre, but this lasted only a few seconds and the signals were unintelligible' (quoted in Middlebrook 1984: 150–51). Apparently reliable reports placed about 100 troops just west of the village, which was indeed exactly where they were supposed to be, en route to their second objective. A few even entered Serre, though what they could now hope to achieve was a mystery, and there was no way to communicate with them. They would be later identified by the brass shoulder titles on their dead bodies (Turner 1993: 153, 168).

On the British side, some of the best work that morning was achieved by the Lewis gunners, one of whom was Pte S.D. Bewsher with the first wave. Bewsher reached as far as a German communication trench, before being stopped and dropping to the ground to return fire:

> I was right in front of a machine gun post. I emptied a drum at a few Germans who were on the trench parapet. They were throwing 'potato-mashers' [stick grenades] over my head – I'd got a bit too near. Some of them went back down the trench – I was surprised to see how wide it was – and I went after them. I got nearly to their second line. I looked around and there was only me there so I decided to go back … I suddenly saw some Germans coming back up their communication trench. I didn't know whether they were picking up wounded or not, I didn't wait to see. I fired at them and they vanished. I was sure they were going to counter attack … I had some narrow squeaks. One bullet hit my water bottle. I felt the water on my leg and I thought it was blood. Another went through my haversack. It broke all my biscuits and hit a tin of bully beef. A piece of shrapnel hit my Lewis gun. It bent the barrel and knocked the foresight clean off. I saw a dead Sheffield Pal with his Lewis gun alongside him. I threw mine down, picked his up and dropped into a shell hole. (Quoted in Turner 1993: 150)

## Hans Amann, Infanterie-Regiment Nr. 169

Born on Christmas Day 1896, young Badener 'lucky' Hans Amann was a soldier of Infanterie-Regiment Nr. 169. Unlike many German troops, Amann was not a conscript, but joined the regiment voluntarily on the wave of popular enthusiasm in August 1914. However, by 1916 he was something of a 19-year-old veteran, his immediate comrades having already been removed by death, wounding, capture or transfer. Eventually surviving four years on the Western Front without injury, he ended the war as a *Vizefeldwebel*, an NCO rank roughly equivalent to sergeant-major. On 1 July 1916, Infanterie-Regiment Nr. 169 expended 74,000 rounds and 1,000 grenades in repelling the 31st Division attack. As one of Amann's comrades, Musketier Karl Blenk, recalled, 'When we started firing we just had to load and reload. They went down in their hundreds. You didn't have to aim, we just fired into them' (quoted in Middlebrook 1984: 157).

Individual Pals who had gone to ground in No Man's Land now began to return fire at those Germans they could see on the enemy parapet. Pte H.C. Bloor of W Company had gone forward in the first wave:

> Eventually I took shelter in a shell hole with two other men from the battalion; we were all wounded. I looked over the edge and could see the Germans in their trench again. I suddenly became very angry. I had seen my battalion mowed down by machine-guns and one of them trapped in the wire … I just couldn't see how any of us would get out of it alive and, so far, I hadn't done anything to the Germans. I made up my mind to get one of them, at least, before I was killed.
>
> I took out my clips of cartridges and laid them out ready for use. I checked the sights on my rifle, settled myself into a comfortable position, took aim and fired. One of the Jerries threw up his arms and fell backwards and the others ducked down. (Quoted in Middlebrook 1984: 162)

Seeing the disintegration of the British attack, Rees decided to intervene:

> My two staff officers, [Capt F.S.G.] Piggott [RE, Rees' Brigade Major] and Stirling, were considerably surprised when I stopped the advance of the rest of the [94th Brigade] machine gun company and certain other small bodies now passing my Headquarters … Messages now began to pour in. An aeroplane reported that my men were in Serre. The Corps and the division urged me to support the attack with all the force at my disposal. I was quite sure that we had not got anyone into Serre except a few prisoners, but the 93rd Brigade on my right reported that their left had got on, whilst the 4th Division beyond them again claimed the first four lines of German trenches and were said to be bombing down our way. (IWM: Doc 77/179/1)

Rees' response to this fragmented information reaching him – and pressure from above to conform to the plan of attack – was to send forward the two companies of 13th York & Lancaster he had retained under his direct control, in order to support the attackers:

> It was obviously necessary to attempt to get a footing in the German front trenches to assist these two attacks. The hostile barrage had eased off by now and was no longer formidable so I ordered two companies of the 13th York and Lancs to make the attempt. I did not know that the German barrage was an observed barrage, but thought it was probably mechanical. As soon as this fresh attack was launched down came the barrage again. One company was badly mauled, whilst the other wisely halted short of it. (IWM: Doc 77/179/1)

Rees was scathing about the direction he received from 31st Division:

> The wildest reports were rife at divisional headquarters at this time. I was ordered to send a company to bomb the Germans out of the front trench of the 93rd Brigade. I expostulated and said that no front trenches existed, but to no purpose. I therefore ordered seventy men near Brigade Headquarters to draw bombs from the dump and take their time about it. A little later I was talking to [Major-]General [R. Wanless-] O'Gowan [GOC 31st Division] and told him that I didn't believe the Germans were in the 93rd's trench at all. He said, to my considerable astonishment, 'Nor do I.' 'In that case,' said I, 'I will stop the attack which you have just ordered me to make' and rushed out of the dugout to cancel the order … When people had recovered from the unbalancing effect of this disaster, I was asked whether I recommended making an attack with the 92nd Brigade [31st Division's reserve infantry brigade on 1 July]. I said 'no', very decidedly. (IWM: Doc 77/179/1)

To expel or exterminate the survivors of 11th East Lancashire involved parts of all three battalions of the Badeners, and co-operation with Reserve-Infanterie-Regiment Nr. 121, as the war diary of Infanterie-Regiment Nr. 169 states:

> As soon as the assault lines broke forward they were met with murderous rifle- and machine gun fire, such that the attack disintegrated before reaching our lines. Only in S2 [the part of the line attacked by 11th East Lancashire], because of the terrain, were the English successful in forcing a way through. After a sharp counter-attack with hand-grenades, however, they were quickly thrown back there as well. Parts of the left- and of the reserve battalions then intervened successfully in the battle in the sector of R.I.R. 121, and there drove the advancing enemy back to a mid-way position. (Jackson 1924)

One German account stated that

> … the British succeeded in making their way through a zone of wrecked wire and trenches and a number of dugouts which had collapsed under the impact of heavy mortar bombs, and they broke into our position where flanks of our 4th and 3rd Companies adjoined. Major Berthold ordered a counter-attack on the part of our I Battalion, and such British as had penetrated our position were driven out again. (Quoted in Duffy 2006: 140)

It took the Germans some time to halt the attack, as was related by Otto Lais:

After the initial confusion and panic caused by our unexpected resistance, after the horrific loss of life in their closely packed attack formations, the English re-form. For two hours and more, wave upon wave breaks against us. With incredible tenacity, they run towards our trenches. In an exemplary show of courage and self-sacrifice, they climb from the safety of their jumping-off position only to be felled, barely having reached our shot-up barbed wire. Twenty, thirty metres in front of our guns, the brave ones fall, the first and the last attack waves together.

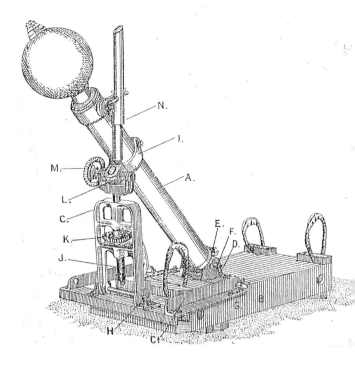

Those following behind take cover behind their dead, groaning and moaning comrades. Many hang, mortally wounded, whimpering in the remains of the barbed wire and upon the hidden iron stakes of the barbed wire barricade. The survivors occupy the slight slope around and behind the remains of the barbed wire and shoot at us like things possessed, without much to aim at. They make cover for themselves from the bodies of their dead comrades and many of us fall in the fire. We shoot into the wire shreds, into the belt of barbed wire that winds to the earth. The hail of bullets breaks up at the wire and strikes downwards as an unpredictable crossfire into the protective slope. Soon the enemy fire dies out here as well.

Fresh waves appear over there, half-emerge from cover then sink again behind the parapets. Officers jump onto the thrown-up earth and try to encourage their men by their example. Flat-helmets emerge in numbers once more only to disappear again immediately. The hail of bullets from our infantry and machine-guns sprays over their defences. (Lais 1935)

Karl Blenk also recalled the scene:

> There was a wailing and lamentation from No Man's Land and much shouting for stretcher-bearers from the stricken English. They lay in piles but those who survived fired at us from behind their bodies. Later on, when the English tried again, they weren't walking this time, they were running as fast as they could but when they reached the piles of bodies they got no farther. I could see the English officers gesticulating wildly, trying to call the reserves forward, but very few came. (Quoted in Middlebrook 1984: 204)

By 0822hrs Rickman was reporting from the British front line that fire was slackening to the front, but from the direction of Gommecourt, to the left, there was still 'heavy machine gun fire', and also occasional bursts from the right. Reports from the front at 0900hrs were that 11th East Lancashire had held the enemy front line for about 20 minutes, 'Bombing Germans back till Bombs were exhausted' (TNA WO 95/2366). Next followed an appeal for reinforcements, a trickle of wounded, and renewed German barrage. Pte Bewsher recalled briefing Rickman on his return from the enemy trenches:

Popularly known as the 'toffee apple bomb thrower', the British 2in mortar was deployed in batteries of four and threw a powerful spherical 50lb projectile 500yd. After the abortive attack of 1 July, Lt-Col Rickman was left holding the British front-line trenches opposite Serre with 50 men, the strongest elements of which were his own headquarters and the trench mortars. Both 2in and light Stokes mortars were present at Serre. Unsurprisingly, he now reported the men 'a good deal rattled', but he stayed at that post until later that evening when wounded by a shell.

There was Colonel Rickman and Lieutenant McAlpine [sic; Lt F.G. Macalpine]. They said, 'Have you just come over, my lad?' I said, 'Yes.' The colonel said, 'Was that you firing over there? Are they Germans?' I said, 'Yes sir, they were just coming down that communication trench, and I felt they were going to counter-attack.' He said, 'You did very well. We've been watching you. Take his name and number, McAlpine!' (Quoted in Levine 2008: 117)

By midday Rickman was preparing for German counter-attack, blocking the trenches with 'bomb stops' and calling for more grenades. For his part, Brig-Gen Rees was well aware what had befallen his brigade:

[Brigadier-]General [J.D.] Ingles [GOC 93rd Brigade] came over to see me early in the afternoon and a member of the corps intelligence branch arrived. I gave the whole lot a lecture on the situation as I saw it and at last convinced my own staff that the whole attack was a terrible failure … We reorganised the remnants of the Brigade to defend our own line. The two leading battalions were annihilated and the two supporting battalions had lost heavily. Out of some 2600 men, who were launched to the attack, very few returned. I had only some 550 men left as far as I could find out …

The result of the timetable in this attack was that it was impossible to alter the artillery barrage before the artillery had completed their programme, owing to the danger of firing on parties of our own troops, who might have got through and be holding the German positions. The cause of failure as far as we were concerned was the skilful assembly by the enemy of a great mass of guns between Serre and Puisieux undetected by us and the concentration of all these guns on a comparatively small, but most important, stretch of front. (IWM: Doc 77/179/1)

Lt-Gen Hunter-Weston put a brave face on disaster, writing to 31st Division on the morning of 2 July that, 'your discipline and determination were magnificent and it was bad luck alone that has temporarily robbed you of success' (quoted in Turner 1993: 172). If Sir Douglas Haig found it impossible to know the scale of losses that morning, the same was true of 94th Brigade. First reports put losses to 11th East Lancashire at 70 killed, 450 wounded and 80 missing, or 83 per cent of those committed to the attack. This figure would subsequently be revised downward to a total of about 585 as survivors reappeared, but the death toll rose to 235. Another 17 died of wounds in the next few weeks. One survivor, L/Cpl F. Sayer, recalled: 'It was a sober moment of time for all of us. About one in five of the original battalion was left and many of these, like me, were not fit for duty … We had trained together for nearly two years and someone had messed things up and we had paid the price' (quoted in Barton 2006: 91).

On the other side of the line, a similar fog of war initially hung over the losses of Infanterie-Regiment Nr. 169, who faced not only the Accrington men, but those of adjoining British battalions. First reports also showed almost 600 casualties, 14 officers and 577 men, of whom nine officers were killed: Oberleutnant Welsch, Oberarzt Dr Schmidt, and Leutnants Schwendemann, Kaufmann, Lehnisch, Beck, Reck, Imle and Hoff. Only later did it prove possible to reduce this very frightening toll to 81 officers and men killed, 151 wounded and ten missing. Moreover, the position was held and there were some prisoners and Lewis guns captured.

# Guillemont

## 30 July 1916

## BACKGROUND TO BATTLE

With hindsight the action of the Pals of 18th Manchester at Guillemont at the end of July was a disaster waiting to happen. The struggle on the Somme continued after 1 July, with the C-in-C Groupe d'armées Nord, Général de division Ferdinand Foch, calling upon the British to support French efforts, and attacks were mounted at Mametz Wood and Contalmaison.

On 1 July the four Manchester Pals battalions of 30th Division had made better progress that day than virtually any other New Army formation. Nevertheless, 16th, 17th and 19th Manchester collectively took several hundred casualties and even the 18th, theoretically in support, was called upon to provide carrying parties and suffered about 175 casualties. On 7 July the first assaults were made at Trônes Wood, quickly involving both 18th and 19th Manchester. Over the next two weeks, all four battalions were ground down in attacks on Trônes, its subsequent defence, and then an assault on Guillemont on 23 July.

Several hundred men and many officers of 18th Manchester were put out of action at Trônes, the commanding officer, Lt-Col W.A. Smith, being killed, temporarily substituted by Maj Phillip Godlee, OC D Company, then replaced by Maj H.B.O. Williams of the 3rd Dragoon Guards. Other casualties included both the Adjutant and the regimental sergeant-major. The battalion did manage a few days out of the line, and received a draft of 440 replacements on 14 July. However, as its history pointed out, this draft was 'lamentably composed':

> ... no less than 27 different regiments were represented. This body consisted almost entirely of private soldiers ... As the battalion was already short of officers and NCOs the training presented a very serious problem ... It became all too

Saxon Reservists in marching order, with packs, leather equipment – officially dyed or polished black from late 1915 – and Gew 98 rifles. Note the Saxon uniform cuff detail with two buttons. The M1895 pack was not usually worn in combat. Pre-war examples were covered in cowhide, complete with hair of varying colours: this gave rise to them being nicknamed *Affe* – monkey, or ape.

clear that the absence of esprit de corps and the lack of officers and NCOs would make discipline in action almost impossible, and so it turned out. (Anon 1923: 209–10)

On 22 July, 18th Manchester was back in the line. Over the next eight days it was shelled intermittently, and took further casualties that had 'the worst possible effect on the troops', making meaningful preparation for forthcoming attack difficult. Nevertheless, accounts by the signal section of 16th Manchester record 'night parades' at Mansell Copse in which attempts were made to practise 'creeping about the countryside like a lot of rabbits, with strict instructions not to make any noise'. These were not judged by participants to be very useful. There was, however, some effort to conduct reconnaissance on the night of 25/26 July, with 90th Brigade mounting three small patrols, one being composed of an officer and two men of 18th Manchester. Each of these parties was briefed by their own commanding officer, and duly dispatched to investigate the front, north to south, in the order that their respective battalions were to attack. The 16th Manchester patrol, supposed to cover the northern sector, got waylaid and emerged from cover to be promptly illuminated by 'continual' enemy flares and harassed by shells: 'practically no information' was obtained.

To the south, the 2nd Royal Scots Fusiliers patrol investigated Arrow Head Copse, before striking out towards Guillemont, reporting 'a good deal of rifle fire and sniping coming from Guillemont'. In the centre of the prospective field of battle, Lt Harrison of 18th Manchester was specifically tasked to discover the condition of the trench marked on the Montauban map as running between Trônes and Guillemont. He climbed into it, discovering that it was only 2ft deep and about 18in wide, then wormed his way in the direction of the enemy, getting to within about 20yd of the German wire. With illuminating flares now falling around him, Harrison felt that further advance would have given away his position, but he did form the impression that there were posts supporting wire directly ahead. The condition of this wire could not be confirmed, but in four places there was also wire crossing the narrow trench, and this he cut. A vigilant enemy had made all three scouting expeditions less than effective, yet there was ample evidence of both strong German presence and wire.

Trench maps corrected to 24 July confirmed what Harrison suspected, showing a double-belt obstacle zone south of the village, and a single belt to the north, doubling again in the vicinity of the station. Whether the acting commanding officer of 18th Manchester, Maj Williams, was able to peruse anything as recent is highly questionable. Little intelligence seems to have permeated to the other ranks.

German sources confirm that the Guillemont sector was held by the Saxons of 24. Reserve-Division, which had arrived early in July, its battalions bolstered with additional machine-gun sections. Also present was Königlich Bayerisches 22. Reserve-Infanterie-Regiment, of 8. Bayerisches Reserve-Division. Rather than cramming forces into front-line trenches, the Germans deployed only three Bavarian companies – 1., 2. and 4. – to the front. The village itself housed the headquarters of the Bavarian I. Bataillon, and of I. Bataillon/Reserve-Infanterie-Regiment Nr. 107. Under the village were concrete dugouts. On the  outskirts lay the headquarters of II. Bataillon/Königlich Sächsisches 9. Infanterie-Regiment Nr. 133. In addition, within striking distance of the village, were more Saxon troops – of Reserve-Infanterie-Regimenter Nr. 104 and Nr. 107, and 2. Reserve-Jäger-Bataillon Nr. 13.

Reserve Infanterie-Regiment Nr. 104 was held in pairs of companies, most as far back as Sailly and the third position, but with Nr. 2 and Nr. 3 under Oberleutnant Truckenbrodt within about 1km (0.6 miles) of the village. Serving with Reserve-Infanterie-Regiment Nr. 104 alongside the regiment's own machine-gun company was Maschinengewehr-Scharfschützen-Trupp Nr. 197. Though the Germans had seen hard service, the three attacking battalions of 90th Brigade would be confronted by not markedly inferior numbers of defenders, spread out, deployed in depth, and copiously equipped with machine guns. Particularly well located were machine-gun teams at Guillemont station, just to the north-west, and at the quarry that fronted the village (Stosch 1927: 209–11).

Troops of both Königlich Sächsisches 5. Infanterie-Regiment 'Kronprinz' Nr. 104 and Reserve-Infanterie-Regiment Nr. 104 man an MG 08. Most are Regulars but at least one man is a Reservist with *Pickelhaube* marked 'R104'. Other details visible here include 1915-type cloth gas-mask bags, loop-hole plates, and the rarely seen large gun shield. Some men wear large 'dragging straps' to help manhandle the gun: communication with the post is by field telephone.

**MAP KEY**

**1 Early morning, 30 July:** Setting off from Brick Lane, 18th Manchester marches through Trônes Wood to its start lines, slowed and confused by gas, fallen trees and shelling.

**2 0345hrs, 30 July:** Last of British attacking force reaches assembly trenches. 18th Manchester re-establishes contact on right with 2nd Royal Scots Fusiliers; other communications are disrupted.

**3 0445hrs, 30 July:** 'Zero hour' – 18th Manchester advances into mist, shelling and machine-gun fire.

**4 0515hrs (approx.), 30 July:** C Company, 18th Manchester seizes the German front-line trench west of Guillemont. The Germans use smoke bombs, and grenade fighting is in progress at the quarry. A Company attempts to assist C Company; D Company strays out of position, coming under fire from the quarry.

**5 0555hrs, 30 July:** Capt F. Wolfenden of B Company, 18th Manchester reports 16th Manchester is not on the left as planned, and asks for reinforcement. Minutes later, 2nd Royal Scots Fusiliers is in Guillemont. At 0630hrs, following 'chaos', 16th Manchester is ordered forward again.

**6 0745hrs, 30 July:** Two companies of 17th Manchester ordered forward with intention of taking the quarry: it is still foggy. Captain P.A. Blythe of C Company, 18th Manchester is reported wounded following close combat at the quarry.

**7 0800hrs, 30 July:** Elements of 18th Manchester reach the western side of Guillemont.

**8 0815hrs, 30 July:** German counter-attacks are put in through Guillemont. Calls for a heavy British barrage are not acted upon for fear of hitting friendly troops. The mist clears: British troops in Guillemont are now cut off to the rear by German bombardment and machine-gun fire. The fight is going badly for the British; attempts to retire at about 0900hrs lead to heavy losses.

**9 1000hrs, 30 July:** The British force remaining on the east side of Trônes Wood is 'badly shaken' by bombardment. No information is received by senior British commanders on troops that penetrated to north and east of Guillemont. 18th Manchester is cut off and under 'bombing attack' from the direction of the station, and the south; constant attempts to resupply the beleaguered British troops with ammunition and grenades are frustrated by the German barrage. By 1100hrs, British commanders are receiving reports that the Germans are working around Arrow Head Copse; the British trenches are systematically shelled. By this point, 2nd Royal Scots Fusiliers and 18th Manchester are now effectively lost.

## Battlefield environment

By late July 1916 Trônes Wood was a mess of shattered trees and human detritus, with Guillemont so heavily bombarded as to be virtually unrecognizable among a moonscape of shell holes. Poor reconnaissance meant the tactical significance of the sunken road to the south went unrecognized, and German machine-gun nests to the north and in the quarry were neither pinpointed, nor neutralized, by the British.

Early-morning mist, a potential advantage for well-prepared attackers, became one more factor alongside gas and damaged communications to make orientation and command extremely difficult. While 18th Manchester and 2nd Royal Scots Fusiliers advanced nearly blind into a cauldron of fire, Reserve-Infanterie-Regiment Nr. 104 and other units were held back, ready to counter-attack should the German front line be penetrated.

A view of Guillemont village as it is now, from the west. (Martin Pegler)

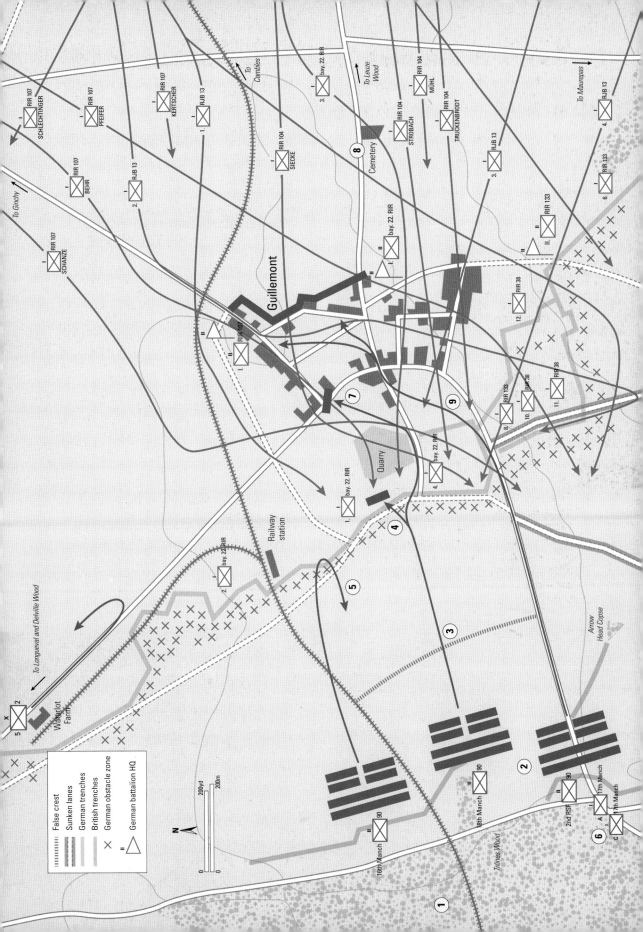

RIR 107
SCHLECHTINGER

RIR 107
PFEIFER

RIR 107
KERTSCHER

RJB 13
1.

To Combles

bay. 22. RIR
3.

To Leuze
Wood

RIR 104
STROBACH

RIR 104
MÜHL

RIR 104
TRUCKENBRODT

To Maurepas

RJB 13
4.

RIR 107
BEHR

RJB 13
2.

RIR 104
SIECKE

Cemetery
8

RIR 104
7.

RJB 13
3.

RIR 133
6.

To Ginchy

RIR 107
SCHANZE

bay. 22. RIR
1.

RIR 133
11.

Guillemont

RIR 107
1.

RIR 38
12.

RJB 38
7

RIR 133
8.

RJB 38
10.

RIR 38
11.

9

bay. 22. RIR

Quarry

bay. 22. RIR
4.

bay. 22. RIR
1.

4

Railway
station

bay. 22. RIR
2.

To Longueval and Delville Wood

5

3

Arrow
Head Copse

Wedgelot
Farm

X
5

2

N

200yd
200m

**False crest**
**Sunken lanes**
**German trenches**
**British trenches**
**German obstacle zone**
X
=  △  **German battalion HQ**

16th Manch
90

18th Manch
90

2

2nd RSF
90

17th Manch
6

17th Manch

A

C

1

Trônes Wood

# INTO COMBAT

Finally came word to 18th Manchester to move out. According to Maj Williams' report,

> The battalion left Brick Lane, the old German front line, and proceeded to the position allotted to them in the assembly trenches east of Trônes Wood … Great difficulty was experienced in this movement as a considerable amount of shelling was taking place. The enemy was using heavy shrapnel, star shells and large quantities of gas shells, which were so overpowering that I gave the order to put on gas helmets. With very few exceptions these gave absolute protection, but it was extremely difficult to see and make headway. (TNA WO 95/2339/3)

The route had been marked in advance with tapes of 'white calico', but there were mishaps and delays. As the 18th Manchester history remarked, the march through Trônes was something never to be forgotten, being made with the 'maximum of discomfort', for 'there are few things more unpleasant than to cross an old battlefield still littered with the wreckage of war in the blackness of the night wearing a gas helmet. Many men after a time took the risk of being gassed rather than endure the pain of constant falls into deep shell holes; many were lost and never took part in the battle' (Anon 1923: 210).

No fewer than 19 attacks had been made here, and the unburied dead numbered in four figures. To make matters worse, many scattered in Trônes Wood were Manchester men, fallen in earlier attacks. As the 18th Manchester picked their way through there was a good deal of straggling, requiring stops for men to close up. Assembly trenches were reached by the last company at 0315hrs. Maj Williams then made two unwelcome discoveries: there was no telephone communication to his headquarters, or with 2nd Royal Scots Fusiliers on the right. Runners were sent out straight away. It would later be determined that buried cables were destroyed by shell fire: pigeons could be used, but visual signalling would be useless until after 0900hrs due to the fog.

Men of the Machine Gun Corps with a Vickers machine gun. This hefty but efficient belt-fed weapon was slightly more modern than the German MG 08, and this example is equipped with a folding light bipod as well as the normal tripod. The crew wear gas helmets – hoods impregnated with neutralizing chemicals – and the firer has the padded waistcoat for carrying the gun on the shoulder. During 18th Manchester's journey to the jump-off positions no fewer than four of the Vickers guns of the accompanying 90th Company, Machine Gun Corps, strayed off course, and two more were destroyed, along with one of the mortars of 90th Trench Mortar Battery.

Nevertheless, at zero hour, 0445hrs, 18th Manchester set off into the mist – in places reducing visibility to less than 40yd – with C and A companies to the fore, left and right, in two lines of platoons, and B and D following in single lines of platoons, so forming third and fourth lines. Pte P. Kennedy recalled: 'There was a heavy ground mist that made direction difficult. Just before the attack, one officer lost an eye and a leg – another had his nose shattered. I bandaged the latter' (IWM: Doc 11098). Not long afterwards, C Company, 18th Manchester under Capt Blythe reached and cleared the trench immediately west of the village, capturing about 100 prisoners. Blythe and his company then moved on to the quarry where they met with 'very heavy' machine-gun fire and both sides threw a 'large quantity' of grenades, 'the enemy also making use of smoke bombs' (TNA WO 95/2339/3).

Oberleutnant Osthelder was killed leading a reserve platoon of the Bavarian regiment in an immediate effort to eject the British. At least part of D Company under 2/Lt F.C.O. Twist lost direction during the advance, straying northward and finding the enemy wire north of the quarry uncut, but having to cross gaps commanded by enemy machine guns led to 'many casualties'. Capt Wolfenden's B Company, which should have had 16th Manchester to its left, was alarmed to discover nothing to its flank, reporting this fact twice, just before 0600hrs and again at 0700hrs. Meanwhile the enemy barrage had restarted, with shells falling in quantity between Guillemont and Trônes. German companies hitherto held back, including those of Reserve-Infanterie-Regiment Nr. 104, were now set in motion, pushing forward into Leuze Wood.

What happened to 16th Manchester could not be determined until much later, but according to the signal section account the battalion managed to get into position by 0330hrs, so were ready to attack at dawn: 'The attack was a failure, and for a time everything was hopeless chaos. Communications were extremely difficult as the shell fire was heavy and continuous. The nervous strain of three big attacks within a month was telling on all those members of the old Section and Battalion who had to go through them' (Anon 1923: 31). The battalion history records that the unit advanced through Bernafay Wood in single file then went forward in 'fog so dense that it was difficult to see more than a few yards ahead'. They hit the railway line using it as a guide, but then walked into machine-gun and rifle fire from both flanks – from both the remains of the railway station, and Guillemont quarry, where enemy machine-gun nests were 'quarried in solid rock'. After several 'gallant attempts' the battalion was withdrawn to a point only slightly in advance of the 'original point of attack'.

All this must have happened quickly, as 90th Brigade's war diary observes that 16th Manchester were back to the British lines before 0630hrs, at which time the battalion's D Company was ordered forward again in an attempt to support 18th Manchester. This also failed, and, under fire, the remains of this company went to ground in shell holes. All co-ordination between 16th and 18th Manchester was lost. This, plus the early crumbling of 2nd Division's effort from the direction of Waterlot Farm, left 18th Manchester entirely unsupported and exposed on their left flank. The action at the quarry now became 'practically hand to hand fighting' and Capt Blythe was wounded: soon, A Company on the right was requested to come to C Company's aid, and moved north. 'While this operation was in progress an order was passed along from the right to retire. No one however appears to know the source from which this order came, and only a small proportion of these companies (about 50 men in all) actually withdrew' (TNA WO 95/2340).

On the battalion's right, things appeared to be going rather better, with Capt Routley still in contact with 2nd Royal Scots Fusiliers, who pushed on into Guillemont, taking 50 prisoners, before repulsing the first of several counter-attacks from the direction of the cemetery. 2nd Royal Scots Fusiliers finally reached as far as the northern edge of Guillemont before halting and losing touch with 18th Manchester, and Routley now arranged for Lt Murray of 2nd Royal Scots Fusiliers to be got to the rear to make a report and request that 'a barrage be kept up on the line of the cemetery and further east to assist consolidation'. This was easier said than done, however, because 'this officer, on his way back to report, saw that the enemy were coming in between him and his battalion, and shot several of them, and had great difficulty in getting back' (TNA WO 95/2340).

An attempt was now made to re-establish control of the quarry, and at about 0730hrs A and C companies of 17th Manchester were ordered up in support, and men who had fallen back went with them. This new impetus allowed 18th Manchester to gain a fresh footing in the western edge of the village. The general situation was deteriorating fast, however, as it was becoming apparent that the attacks on both flanks of 90th Brigade had failed, and the further forward the two lead battalions went, the greater the danger they would be lost. Orders were given that the lead elements should consolidate on the western edge of the village while bombardment was laid on a line 200yd east of the church. This made sense, but getting orders through was all but impossible, 'as patrols sent forward to the village either did not return, or could not get near enough to find out the situation'. The fog still being thick, direction was lost and supports strayed north coming under heavy enfilading rifle and machine-gun fire.

At 0815hrs the Germans were reported to be 'counter attacking through the village'. Companies of Reserve-Infanterie-Regiment Nr. 107, led by Leutnants Schanze, Behr, Pfeifer, Schlechtinger and Kertscher, were attempting to relieve the Bavarians, and secure their own battalion headquarters, though the strength of the British remained 'undetermined'. Foremost in combat were Unteroffizier Wünsche, Gefreiter Pilz and Soldat Schaefer, 'advancing in leaps and bounds, incessantly throwing hand grenades'. Despite the death of Pilz, these men managed to overcome one of the British Lewis teams and capture an officer. Under machine-gun fire, Soldat Naumann, bobbing from shell hole to shell hole, re-established contact with Königliche Bayerische Reserve-Infanterie-Regiment Nr. 22. That regiment's 3. Kompagnie, hitherto held back on the eastern side of Guillemont, was now also able to push forward using four sections, and a *Stoss* or shock troop led by Gefreiter Reimer. Soon the fight would also be joined by two companies of Reserve-Jäger-Bataillon Nr. 13, one platoon of which managed to fight its way diagonally through Guillemont between the positions of 18th Manchester and 2nd Royal Scots Fusiliers (Stosch 1927: 211–15).

Historians of the Manchester Pals complain that at this crucial juncture support from artillery was limited to a few field guns and was completely inadequate. However, the 90th Brigade war diary records that British troops were reported 'north and north west' of the village: the barrage was lifted accordingly onto the German trench east of the cemetery. Tragically, it appears that the lapse between messages being sent from Guillemont and artillery reaction was precluding all effective co-operation, with shelling being directed away from last recorded British positions on the strength of out-of-date reports. The remaining men of 18th Manchester were now trapped, fighting between machine-gun fire to the fore, and barrage to the rear, out of contact with all – including the commanding officer.

Despite the clearing of the fog the Pals now found 'it was impossible to keep communication with the troops in Guillemont village owing to the heavy MG and artillery fire between the village and Trônes Wood' (Anon 1923: 211–212). With little artillery support and great difficulty bringing up grenades from the rear the Manchester men were forced to rely upon Lewis guns and rifles. As Pte Kennedy recalled of a similar situation, chargers of ammunition were taken out of pouches and laid on the parapet – 'a good tip because I could load very, very quickly and fire' (IWM: Doc 11098). By 0900hrs the fight was going badly; according to the commanding officer's report, an order was given by an unknown officer to fall back, and the troops attempted to comply, but in doing so suffered 'very heavily'. At 1000hrs it was clear to Maj Williams that not only were the men holding the east side of Trônes Wood 'badly shaken', but that the remainder of 2nd Royal Scots Fusiliers and 18th Manchester were cut off by both the enemy bombardment and enemy infantry, who delivered bombing attacks south from Guillemont station, and north from the trenches in front of 89th Brigade, where the attack of the Liverpool Pals had already faltered – though a strong point just south of Arrow Head Copse had been taken.

On the eastern edge of the village the counter-attacking companies of Reserve-Infanterie-Regiment Nr. 104, under Oberleutnant Siecke and Leutnants Truckenbrodt and Mühl, faced heavy British artillery fire. Siecke was badly wounded, and Leutnant Hennig killed. Leutnant Röhler, who had already distinguished himself on 23 July, assumed command. Nevertheless, with 2nd Royal Scots Fusiliers surrounded by other units and reduced to only a handful of effectives, the new German assault was able to penetrate the village from the east, and emerging from the western side, meet the trenches formerly occupied by the Bavarians. Here 91 British – including two officers – were captured. Having personally taken a machine gun Roehler swung southwards, in association with Heinemann's and Pfeifer's companies of Reserve-Infanterie-Regiment Nr. 107, towards the sunken road south-west of

The unit of the man shown here, Infanterie-Regiment 'Grossherzog Friedrich von Baden' (8. Württembergisches) Nr. 126, served on the Somme from October 1916 with 39. Infanterie-Division, having suffered casualties equivalent to 69 per cent of its strength at Verdun earlier in the year. The *Stahlhelm* was introduced experimentally at Verdun and was in general issue to front-line troops on the Somme. Unteroffizier Georg Bucher got his first steel helmet, and much else, on arrival in the sector: 'I had been determined, ever since we left Villiers, to get hold of one of those steel buckets: I therefore decided to take my party across to the concrete cabins, where an artillery NCO graciously dispensed, for a suitable consideration, steel helmets, hand grenades, gas masks, dixies, breech blocks, and so on … The things are worth their weight in gold' (Bucher 2006: 106).

A Saxon infantryman throwing a *Stielhandgranate*. Introduced in 1915, the stick grenade was ignited by means of a pull cord running through the handle, and exploded after a 5½-second delay, relying mainly on blast rather than fragmentation. As soldiers disappeared into the earth of the 'empty battlefield', grenades became ever more important, as was reported by Leutnant Matthäus Gerster of Reserve Infanterie-Regiment Nr. 119: 'The importance of the hand grenade in close quarter battle was repeatedly drummed into every single man … They were shown how to beat off attacks, by using masses of grenades simultaneously … The technique of bombing from traverse to traverse to wrest back, bit by bit from the enemy, a trench which he had forced his way into, was also demonstrated. Each man had to throw live grenades' (quoted in Sheldon 2005: 83–84).

Guillemont. In this phase the attackers 'vied with each other in courage' during the final mopping up, with the Bavarian troops alone counting 100 prisoners. In the British official account it was Infanterie-Regiment Nr. 104 that assisted in 'restoring' the position, armed resistance continuing as late as 1400hrs (Stosch 1927: 216–20; Miles 1938: 165–66).

The desperate remains of 18th Manchester had no way to communicate but by runners, attempting to brave a veritable storm of fire: most did not get through. As the Victoria Cross citation of CSM George Evans of B Company relates, this 2nd Anglo-Boer War veteran volunteered for the job after five other runners had been killed. Remarkably, CSM Evans was already 40 years old, having previously displayed 'great bravery and devotion to duty' in battle at Montauban and Trônes Wood:

> … he had to cover about 700 yards, the whole of which was under observation of the enemy. Company Sergeant Major Evans, however succeeded in delivering the message, and although wounded, rejoined his company, although advised to go to the dressing station. The return journey to the Company again meant a journey of 700 yards under severe rifle and machine gun fire, but by dodging from shell hole to shell hole he was able to do so. (Anon 1923: 212)

Few men of 17th Manchester who had come up in support of 18th Manchester made it back again. Lt Alan Holt recalled:

> I got up to the village in the mist with my men without casualties, but after spending three hours there and losing a lot of men we were ordered to retire. It was then daylight and the mist had lifted: we had to walk back over 800 yards of open ground, and how I got back I don't know; very few of my men did, as we were

swept by two machine guns. I got a machine gun bullet through the sole of my boot, another through the holster of my revolver, also a piece of shell which went through the holster and smashed the handle of my revolver on the way. Just as we were leaving the village I was hit in the back with a small piece of shrapnel, but it is nothing serious and I was able to carry on till the Brigade was relieved on Monday morning. (Quoted in Stedman 2004: 150)

Those who could not retire during the afternoon were the dead, wounded and captured, but sometimes failing light offered men trapped out in No Man's Land a welcome opportunity to escape. After dusk Williams waited for stragglers and wounded to arrive at headquarters. Only eight or ten did so. As was so often the case it was barrages, or the lack of them, that shaped the infantry battle. Machine-gunner Unteroffizier Georg Bucher fought on the same sector at about this time, witnessing British attacks from the south:

There was still much work to be done and we had to clear the dead out of the way. Suddenly the shell fire came down on us with diabolical fury: we were being ripened for the Tommies' attack. Two hours later they advanced under cover of a moving barrage – thin lines of steel helmeted figures. Our fire devoured them greedily. Fresh lines came on and were devoured – still more and more came on. Either they were utterly careless of death or else, what was far more likely, they had been doped with whisky. Yet they couldn't reach us. Then our barrage came down – no barrage could have been more intense or more compact. That stopped the Tommies, and they 'went to earth' in a line of shell holes right among the heaped up bodies of their dead. Once more their artillery fire broke over us with infernal noise and intensity, but that could not restore to life the hundreds of their dead. An hour later the attack was resumed, not far off on our left, with the result that our flank was exposed. A desperate counter attack restored the situation – the English were literally hacked to bits. The carnage was unbelievable, so too was the English bravery. (Bucher 2006: 119)

The appalling disaster at Guillemont was given just nine lines in the main volume of the 18th Manchester war diary. Two of these were taken up with the bald statement '14 officers, and 470 other ranks killed, wounded and missing'. The 1923 battalion history lists seven officers killed at Guillemont, and 98 other ranks who died on 30 July, plus at least one who 'died of wounds' the next day. Most of the remainder were wounded or taken prisoner. It is interesting to note that 16th Manchester suffered eight officer casualties of whom all but one died, or died of their wounds, but the far lower total of 194 other-rank casualties, including killed, wounded and missing. Given the 18th Manchester account it seems very possible that 16th Manchester broke relatively rapidly. 2nd Royal Scots Fusiliers all but ceased to exist, with 17 officers and 633 other ranks out of action; at least 204 members of the regiment died in the 48 hours commencing with the morning of 30 July, the vast majority falling at Guillemont, and having no known graves. Losses to 90th Brigade totalled 1,463. After the action at Guillemont some of the prisoners were assembled at Moislains, where they were seen by General der Artillerie Max von Gallwitz, Below's successor at 2. Armee and also commander of the *Armeegruppe* that bore his name:

# Clash at Guillemont

**BRITISH VIEW:** Bombardment, mist, limited reconnaissance, machine-gun fire, indifferent planning and damaged communications made it surprising that any British troops reached the remains of Guillemont. Nevertheless, 2nd Royal Scots Fusiliers and 18th Manchester captured the front-line trenches of Königlich Bayerisches 22. Reserve-Infanterie-Regiment and penetrated the village. They were entirely out of command and communication range, with enemy bombardment falling behind them.

Here, 18th Manchester has advanced a Lewis gun team on the right, but are already short of officers and NCOs, and lacking sufficient grenades. Many troops have been with the unit for only a couple of weeks. Calls for artillery support have failed as runners are killed, and command refrains from acting owing to its fears that misplaced British bombardment will hit friendly troops. Few men of 18th Manchester escaped the debacle. After the battle another draft of 507 men would be required to rebuild the battalion.

**GERMAN VIEW:** From the German point of view we see an MG 08 on improvised 'trench mount' has been pushed up to give covering fire as men of Reserve-Infanterie-Regiment Nr. 104, wearing 'assault packs', emerge from dugouts and cellars to advance by grenade throwing and rushes from shell hole to shell hole. In a series of small counter-attacks, 2nd Royal Scots Fusiliers would be all but annihilated and 18th Manchester progressively surrounded.

As the British *Official History* put it, speaking of the enemy situation, '… the battle area had developed and completely altered fighting conditions. Troops lay in shell holes more difficult than trenches for the enemy artillery to locate; but existence in crater defences made enormous demands on the physique and spirit of the men and made it very difficult to exercise command, distribute supplies, and care for the wounded. Unburied dead infected the air and took away the desire to eat; warm food could be brought up only at night and seldom reached the front positions, where the troops existed on tinned provisions; there was great lack of water in the summer heat' (Miles 1938: 172).

... all khaki brown, wearing those saucer shaped helmets of theirs, with typically British sharp faced features beneath ... It was enlightening to learn about the results of interrogations and conversations with the thirty British prisoners taken on the 29th and 30th. They included recruits who had only just arrived at front line units, and who had been under fire for the first time. In neither appearance or intelligence did they make the same good impression as the men of the first Kitchener divisions. (Quoted in Duffy 2006: 204–05)

The battered remains of rolling stock at Guillemont station amid a featureless landscape. German machine-gun posts around here flanked the British attackers on 30 July, creating beaten zones and making advance and retreat equally difficult.

Reserve-Infanterie-Regiment Nr. 104 had suffered 127 casualties, of whom 99 were wounded. It was, according to the German account, 'a special day of honour for Saxony and Bavaria'. However, 24. Reserve-Division losses totalled 1,653 on 30 July, more than half of these falling within 90th Brigade's sector. Between 14 and 31 July, in the face of repeated attacks, the ten infantry battalions of 24. Reserve-Division suffered 5,476 casualties.

Following the attack, Maj-Gen J.S.M. Shea, GOC 30th Division, put on a positive gloss, claiming that while Guillemont had not been taken, the attack was a success because it broke up an impending counter-attack on Trônes Wood. This is difficult to substantiate, and indeed by the time of the writing of the *Official History* the engagement was accepted as not just a failure, but the sort of action that could be held up as stereotypically short-sighted:

It is little matter for surprise that the attack made on 30th July should have taken almost the exact course of the action of the 23rd: the conditions under which it was delivered were practically the same. After the first experience it seemed to local commanders that an assault against the Guillemont positions from the west – up the exposed shallow trough which marked the termination of Caterpillar Valley – and from the south-west – over a crest and down a slope, both devoid of cover – had little chance of success ... the results of 30 July could hardly be viewed with satisfaction; again very little progress had been made, and that only as the result of

German dead in the sunken lane, Guillemont. According to Maj Rowland Feilding of 6th Battalion, The Connaught Rangers, in September 1916, 'It is almost literally true to say that not a brick or stone [in Guillemont] remains intact. Indeed, not a brick or stone is to be seen, except it is churned up by a bursting shell ... There is nothing but the mud and the gaping shell holes – a chaotic wilderness of shell holes, rim overlapping rim' (quoted in Powell 2006: 173).

very heavy casualties and of a great expenditure of ammunition. The Germans, who now held their front lightly, their troops being distributed in depth, continued to resist with great obstinacy ... As ever, the machine gun played a great part in the defence ... (Miles 1938: 165–67)

As Haig himself observed, 'The only conclusion that can be drawn from the repeated failure of attacks on Guillemont is that there is something wanting in the methods employed'. One reason for Guillemont's apparent impregnability was discovered when it finally fell. As a private letter reprinted in a 30th Division report of 9 September explained, it was partly a matter of deceptive topography:

I was in Guillemont yesterday and you will doubtless be interested to hear something of the sunken road, the road in a deepish cutting and the edges of the slopes are flush with the surrounding ground and you cannot see the road until you are right on to it, the Boshes had entrenched it and had made a number of very rough dugouts under the bank, and the bank of the road was lined with rifle pits. I saw no less than four machine guns in a length of 150 yards or so, no special emplacements, the guns having simply been fitted into a niche near the top of the slope so as to just clear the ground. No wire at all in front of the road. Not a great deal of damage to the road from shell fire, in fact extraordinarily little compared with the surrounding ground, and it seemed to me that the mystery of Guillemont lay in the fact that the sunken road was just below a fold in the ground and not under observation, and that whilst Guillemont itself got heavily shelled, the sunken road itself escaped very largely ... (30th Division War Diary, TNA WO 95/2325)

# Thiepval

## 26–27 September 1916

## BACKGROUND TO BATTLE

Thiepval, standing on a modest ridge in the German front line, had been a British objective on the first day of the Somme battle. Yet while 36th (Ulster) Division briefly penetrated the nearby Schwaben Redoubt, neither the Ulstermen nor 32nd Division were able to take Thiepval with its interconnected cellars and bunkers protected by machine-gun nests that both flanked the front and swept across the village, and the supporting German artillery batteries pre-registered on Thiepval Wood. Over the following three months the village resisted both attack and bombardment, as thousands of shells transformed the ruins of château, church, brewery and houses into a rubble-strewn subterranean strongpoint, dotted with broken trees.

As obstacle zone and front-line trenches were progressively battered, the German garrison, I. Bataillon/ Infanterie-Regiment Nr. 180, became increasingly reliant on bombing parties, known as *Handgranatentruppen*, drawn from its companies to repel close attack. Though there was a constant stream of casualties – mainly from shells and gas – and communication cables destroyed, German defensive successes were also scored, as when in early September

Archaeologically re-excavated trenches in Thiepval Wood, with replacement sandbags and duck-boards. From these trenches, men of 36th (Ulster) Division began their attack on 1 July by creeping out into No Man's Land before zero hour. A relatively successful assault was achieved by taking advantage of cover in a sunken road, and not pausing to form up. Nevertheless, by the end of the day the Ulstermen had suffered heavy casualties and were forced to give up almost all their gains.

raids were mounted and at least 11 Lewis guns captured. On 10 September Major Weeber assumed command of the battalion.

*Minenwerfer* (trench mortars) had been deployed at Thiepval since 1915. As was remarked by Leutnant Gerster of Reserve-Infantry-Regiment Nr. 119:

> The long period of positional warfare brought with it a thorough reorganisation and an increase in the means of close quarter battle. Heavy and medium mortars had proved their worth everywhere where the trenches were near to one another. This was the case at Thiepval, where there was much patrol activity and the accumulation of mortars served the tactical purpose of destroying obstacles and enemy trenches … Old makeshift light mortars disappeared to be replaced by the *Lanz* mortars, which proved to have a long range and be easily transportable. In August the earth mortars with which the 28th Reserve Division had had good experiences near La Boisselle, made their first appearance in the brigade area. These were the old type with guide rails, upon which the beer barrel type rounds were launched steeply towards the enemy … (Quoted in Sheldon 2005: 79)

By summer 1916 the old mortars at Thiepval had been replaced by Albrecht types. These were wooden barrelled, reinforced with wire winding and metal clamps. Though not very accurate, they threw a 240mm round up to 550m.

Microscopic and hugely expensive as they were, Entente advances since the opening of the battle had changed the tactical situation at Thiepval. Successive pushes towards Pozières made a threatening mile-deep bulge in the front line, creating a suggestion of that holy grail of trench warfare, a flank, where formerly the village had been a brick in a solid wall. Accordingly, Thiepval now formed a small salient, subject to crossfire and apparently vulnerable to being crushed. So it was that the late-September battle for Thiepval Ridge was conceived, with British 18th and 11th divisions, and Canadian 1st and 2nd divisions, tasked with advancing broadly northwards on a 6,000yd front, following a barrage of 800 guns.

The crucial task of 18th (Eastern) Division was the clearance of Thiepval, led by Lt-Col F.A. Maxwell VC's 12th (Service) Battalion, The Duke of Cambridge's Own (Middlesex Regiment), of 54th Brigade. The plan was to advance in bounds to three objective lines in turn, with a 15-minute halt on the first, just below the crest, and a pause of one hour on the second. The battalion's right would rest on 53rd Brigade, also of 18th Division; from the left, machine guns of 49th (West Riding) Division played on the German front line. The British artillery barrage was of the 'step by step' type, and was to be 'followed as closely as possible'. So 12th Middlesex could advance unimpeded, 'clearing parties' of 11th (Service) Battalion, The Royal Fusiliers (also of 54th Brigade) were allotted to mopping up between the front line and the second objective. Even so, it would be 7th (Service) Battalion, The Bedfordshire Regiment – the 'Shiny Seventh' – who would participate in the climax of the struggle for Thiepval.

C Company, 12th Middlesex, led on the right, with B on its left: D was in support, and A in reserve. D Company was to dispose itself behind the main attack with bombing sections and Lewis guns to the fore; A Company was to be ready to reinforce the assault companies, looking for any gaps to exploit or fill. The second wave was to catch up with the first, on the first objective, and the third and fourth waves halt at least 100yd behind. Bombers were to be deployed alongside enemy trenches, but used 'only in emergency'. Each man was to carry 170 rounds and two grenades, bombers ten bombs in canvas 'bomb buckets' and 50 rounds. Water bottles were filled with cold tea and large packs were to be deposited in a battalion dump.

The advance would be made in 'artillery formation' – that is, spread out enough to diminish the effects of enemy guns; 'No man is to get into the enemy's front or second line trench but carry on at steady pace – those men nearest to the trenches firing into them if necessary. Each wave will have two bombers behind the men next to these two enemy front trenches' (TNA: WO 95/2044). Interestingly, two Vickers guns from 54th Company, Machine Gun Corps were attached to 12th Middlesex, and two light trench mortars devoted to support. Upon the barrage lifting, 12th Middlesex's attack would proceed to the second objective, B Company moving its two Lewis guns to outflank the enemy left, while the third and fourth waves halted on the road behind. This achieved, A and D companies were to take over as assaulting companies, pushing on all the way into the Schwaben Redoubt. Lt-Col Maxwell issued a morale-raising message immediately prior to the attack:

The 'Die Hards' have a great chance today: viz – to take Thiepval, which has defied the efforts of all other regiments, brigades and divisions for three months. We must do it, and we will do it 'on our heads', as the enemy is demoralised, we have enormous superiority of guns, and all of us are out to kill, and reach our objective … Tanks are due to cooperate with us today. It may not be an easy job, but if it is tough we can carry it through if we keep going: don't stop and don't retire one yard. Be out to kill and get Thiepval on our colours. (TNA: WO 95/2044)

## INTO COMBAT

The British assault commenced with a stroke of good luck. A brisk departure from the front-line trench meant that the German artillery barrage – intended to smash the attack before it had started, overshot, catching only some of

Thiepval from the air, with shells bursting on German positions. Many individual trenches can be picked out, such as Schwaben-Graben, running horizontally through the thick of the bombardment, and, parallel to the north, Hoher-Steg, about the centre of the image.

Men of The Border Regiment rest in small 'funk holes' dug under the forward lip of a trench in Thiepval Wood, August 1916. Details visible include a set of 1914 Pattern leather equipment, groundsheets, and to the left, the 1914-type winter cap and steel helmet in sacking cover.

**MAP KEY**

**1** **1235hrs, 26 September:** 'Zero hour'. Hard on the heels of bombardment, 12th Middlesex attacks, its first wave suffering serious casualties from machine-gun fire.

**2** **1250hrs (approx.), 26 September:** 12th Middlesex passes through German front lines, supported by two tanks; one fails to get to Thiepval, the other reaches the château. 12th Middlesex's right wing makes good progress, but the left slows against the village strongpoint. The second tank is ditched at about 1300hrs.

**3** **1430hrs, 26 September:** 12th Middlesex reports its arrival on second objective, beyond the village, the north-west part of which is still in German hands. Even so, by 1520hrs – at which time 54th Brigade HQ receives a message, by pigeon – 12th Middlesex and 11th Royal Fusiliers, to its left, are now 'practically expended'.

**4** **1730hrs, 26 September:** Infanterie-Regiment Nr. 180 holds Martinspfad with the assistance of Infanterie-Regiment Nr. 66. At 1755hrs, British 18th Division HQ suspends the action.

**5** **0600hrs, 27 September:** Having commenced the attack with the coming of daylight, 15 minutes earlier – without bombardment, and using 'bomb and bayonet' – C Company, 7th Bedfordshire is engaged in bomb duels in the German position.

**6** **0650hrs, 27 September:** D Company, 7th Bedfordshire's attack is under way on the left; at 0700hrs 7th Bedfordshire personnel commence bombing along the German trenches, clearing the dugouts and capturing the remaining part of the village by 0800hrs.

**7** **0930hrs, 27 September:** Reserve-Leutnant Kimmich reports just 100 men of Infanterie-Regiment Nr. 180 are left in Hoher-Steg.

## Battlefield environment

On 23 September I. Bataillon/Infanterie-Regiment Nr. 180 remained ensconced beneath Thiepval. The cramped battlefield was now a claustrophobic area of rubble and tree-stumps, traversed by trenches intended mainly to resist attack from the west. As Reserve-Leutnant Kimmich wrote in his diary on 21 September: 'Picture a desert, the entire country without one green blade of grass, everything ploughed up by shells. In the line itself no one knows who the other is, neither we nor the English knows for certain where the nearest opponent is. Every foot of ground is prepared for battle. One cannot move without a gas mask, everywhere smells of rotten apples to such an extent that one's eyes water and one's nose also in sympathy is affected' (quoted in Barton 2006: 250).

On 26 September 12th Middlesex attacked with partial success, but were exhausted by evening. The relatively fresh 7th Bedfordshire would manage to get into position close to the German defenders during the night, the British sheltering much of their strength in captured bunkers, but hopes of assault before dawn were frustrated. Despite the linear nature of the attack plan, 7th Bedfordshire wasted as little time as possible crossing dangerous open terrain, focusing on entering trenches and clearance by bombing teams. Wise as such tactics were, much was demanded of junior leaders whose tiny battles were fought out of touch with higher command. With disadvantage of numbers, limited supply of munitions and severely disrupted communications, the final question was how many men the few remaining German leaders could extract.

A view of present-day Thiepval, from the ridge next to Mouquet Farm on the road leading in from Pozières Ridge. (Martin Pegler)

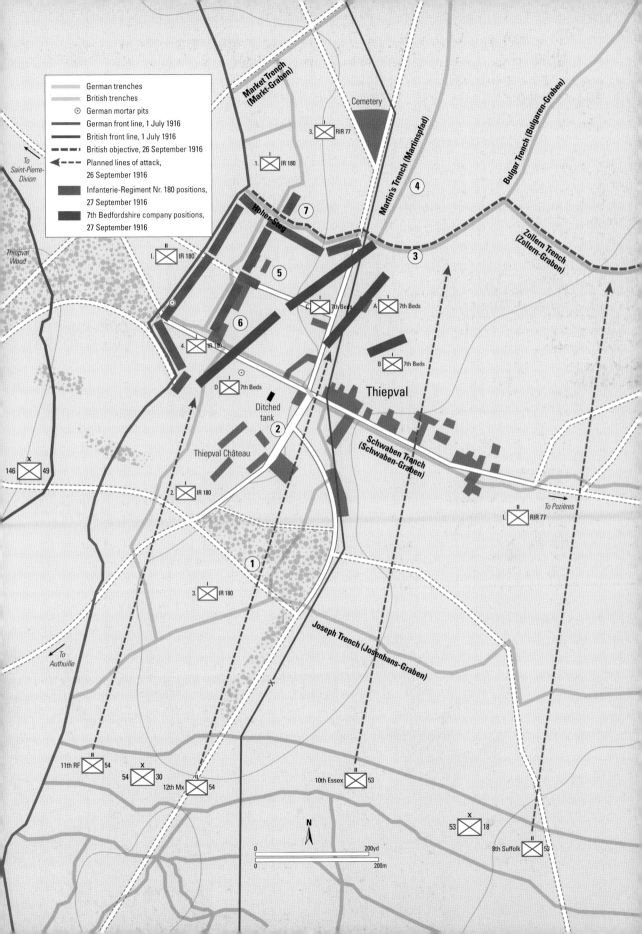

**Legend:**

| | |
|---|---|
| | German trenches |
| | British trenches |
| ⊙ | German mortar pits |
| | German front line, 1 July 1916 |
| | British front line, 1 July 1916 |
| ---- | British objective, 26 September 1916 |
| ◄---- | Planned lines of attack, 26 September 1916 |
| | Infanterie-Regiment Nr. 180 positions, 27 September 1916 |
| | 7th Bedfordshire company positions, 27 September 1916 |

To Saint-Pierre-Divion

Market Trench (Markt-Graben)

Cemetery

3. RIR 77

1. IR 180

Martin's Trench (Martinspfad)

Bulgar Trench (Bulgaren-Graben)

④

Hoher-Steg

⑦

Zollern Trench (Zollern-Graben)

③

Thiepval Wood

I. IR 180

⑤

⊙

⑥

C 7th Beds   A 7th Beds

4. IR 180

B 7th Beds

D 7th Beds

⊙

Thiepval

Ditched tank

② Thiepval Château

146 ✕ 49

2. IR 180

Schwaben Trench (Schwaben-Graben)

To Pozières

I. RIR 77

① 

3. IR 180

To Authuille

Joseph Trench (Josenhans-Graben)

11th RF ‖ 54

54 ✕ 30

12th Mx ‖ 54

10th Essex ‖ 53

N

53 ✕ 18

8th Suffolk ‖ 53

0        200yd
0        200m

11th Royal Fusiliers, a platoon of which was witnessed 'buried' by Lt-Col Maxwell. This luck would not last long, however, and German sources would claim the first wave almost destroyed. As Maxwell put it:

> During the advance all casualties occurred from machine gun and rifle fire, the great bulk of them from machine guns firing from the old German front line trenches, and many from another one or two posted at the Chateau. Just beyond the Chateau line, heavy Minenwerfer also came into play, a cannister destroying as many as four or five men at a time. When passing or clearing dugouts casualties also occurred from bombs, which the enemy used freely. His bombs were of the 'Jam Pot' and 'Egg' variety, but generally speaking their killing powers seem to be much less than those of our 'Mills' bombs. Practically no enemy was seen with bayonets attached to their rifles. (TNA: WO 95/2044)

As Philip Gibbs reported for the *Daily Sketch* of 28 September:

> It was on the left that our men had the hardest time. One battalion [12th Middlesex], leading the assault, had to advance directly upon the chateau – that heap of rubbish, and from cellars beneath it came waves of savage machine gun fire. They were also raked by an enfilade fire of machine guns from the top left corner of the ground where the village once stood. Our men were astounded, 'I didn't believe it was possible,' said one of them, 'that any living soul could be there after all that shell fire, but blessed, as soon as it switched off, if the Germans did not come up like rabbits out of bunny holes, and fire most hellishly.'

A British stretcher party out 'over the top' at Thiepval; German grenades, bandoliers and loop-hole plates are littered around. Lightly wounded men were expected to find their own way to the regimental aid post, but more severely wounded men had to wait for the stretcher-bearers. Although the British medical services had considerable experience of dealing with gunshot wounds, the appalling injuries inflicted by shells proved even more destructive. In the first 24 days of the Somme battle, 136,000 British personnel became casualties, testing the medical services to the limit.

Of the two tanks allotted to the attack the female, C2 *Cognac*, ditched before it could reach Thiepval. However, the male, C5 *Crème de Menthe*, succeeded in getting into action, though somewhat belatedly, coming in behind – rather than in front of, or with – the main assault. Much of its fire was, therefore, over the heads of 12th Middlesex. Nevertheless, it did good work around the château and even advanced beyond it before ditching in a shell hole. This was alarming as its machine guns suddenly depressed, and some of the infantry were hit. Moreover, 'it also undoubtedly crushed wounded who were lying deep in shell holes, and therefore could not be seen'. The *Daily Sketch* glossed over the more hideous details: 'A tank had been coming along slowly in a lumbering way, crawling over the interminable succession of shell craters, lurching over, and down, and into and out of old German trenches; nosing heavily into the soft earth, and grinding up again, and sitting poised on broken parapets, as though quite winded by this exercise, and then waddling forward in the wake of the infantry.'

According to a report in the *Manchester Guardian*, the Germans attacked the stranded tank, swarming around it 'like bees':

> They displayed extraordinary courage. Although the hidden batteries of the vehicle showered them with fire, they attempted with desperate violence to storm the

mobile armoured fort and to kill its crew. Despite ceaseless machine gun fire, they helped one another to climb onto the steel roof. They obviously hoped to find hatches and cracks in the monster's armour, but they might as well have been attacking a battleship with spades. It was an indescribable sight, this battle of man against machine. The crew on the inside were filled with fury. Not in their wildest dreams had they considered it possible they might be attacked. These Germans were driven on by blind determination. In the madness of the moment, they were willing to stake their lives. Finally the British infantry attacked and drove them back.

Relations between Lt-Col Maxwell and Capt Arthur Inglis, *Crème de Menthe*'s commander, soured when the latter fretted about possible capture of his machine after it became immobilized. There was, however, little reason to question Inglis's personal bravery, for only a fortnight earlier he had been awarded an immediate Distinguished Service Order for conspicuous gallantry during the first tank attack, during which *Crème de Menthe* had continued battering German machine-gun posts within the Courcelette sugar factory with her 6-pdr guns despite shell damage. Efforts to shift *Crème de Menthe* at Thiepval that night failed, and a photograph shows that at some stage she lost half her steering gear. The tank was, therefore, left where she was, later serving as a signal station.

Despite these problems, Maxwell remained convinced that the support of the tank 'was of the greatest value', and the fight continued. Platoons now pushed their way along what had once been the front line, bombing out the enemy who frantically created one *Barrikade* – or bomb stop across the trench – after another:

British Mk I 'male' tank moving up. The original press caption states that this picture was taken on 25 September, and depicts one of the machines deployed to Thiepval, though this has been questioned. Note the netting on a wooden frame to prevent grenades exploding on the relatively vulnerable top decking. At this stage tanks were a terrifying novelty for the German infantry, and a significant local factor, but short range and unreliability prevented them from realizing their full effectiveness.

At two dug outs particularly there was close fighting, our men using the bayonet. One young man (Pte Stubbs) fighting splendidly beside his brother (a Sergt) had his leg shattered by a bomb, but continued fighting with a revolver he picked up. He died very soon, his brother also being killed … Stubborn parties of the enemy were dealt with by Lewis guns, also others when retreating along trenches or in the open. At dusk an enemy reinforcement of from 90 to 100 men were seen coming down the hill (and therefore in full view) along Martins Lane [König-Strasse]. The word was passed down, and a machine gun, a Lewis gun, and every man who could see into the trench was laid on it, and the enemy appeared to be completely annihilated. (TNA WO 95/2044)

On the second objective there was a nasty surprise when Maj Whinney and a small group of men suddenly came under fire at close range. They were all killed except a sergeant, whose rifle was damaged by a bullet, and who was promptly dragged underground by a German officer brandishing a pistol. Having been briefly questioned, the British sergeant was left in the charge of a sentry; the following day he was abandoned when the Germans retreated, and rejoined his unit.

The operation was declared a success, and it was claimed that 12th Middlesex had taken Thiepval. Any celebration was, however, premature. Among others of his brigade, 2/Lt Henry Cartwright of 7th (Service) Battalion, The Bedfordshire Regiment, waited in trepidation for the verdict:

All day we waited expectantly, knowing that if the attack did not succeed we should be called up, and I am not above admitting that success might be obtained without our aid. It was not to be though. About midnight the order came for us to move up to the Chateau. We had no guides, and the country was foreign to us. What a journey it was! The left half Company lost the right half, and every moment we expected to walk into the hands of the Bosche. However as so often happens in these cases we did at last hit the Chateau, and we soon knew it for the Hun shelled it to blazes.

Captain [T.R.] Mulligan [OC D Company] met us there, and we learnt that 'C' and 'D' Companies would attack at 5 am (it was then 4.30 am) on the sound of a whistle. There would be no artillery support, and we were to creep over and endeavour to capture the remainder of the village by surprise. We were extended in shell holes and our direction pointed out, and then began an interminable wait. Gradually dawn broke, and still no whistle blew. A tank embedded in a shell hole attempted to move, and we thought 'now is the time', but it stuck fast, and after many attempts to move at last gave up the attempt. It drew light, and I went along the line to chat with [2/Lt Henry] Potts and Major Merrick. It was then the whistle blew and I hurried back to my platoon. (Quoted in Deacon 2004: 119)

If the men of 7th Bedfordshire were anxious about the impeding attack on the other side of the line, I. Bataillon/Infanterie-Regiment Nr. 180 was already in a perilous situation; the German unit now occupied a small tongue of land, originally part of the front line, and were attacked from what was formerly the flank and rear. From the front there was still harassment across the old No Man's Land of 1 July. The battalion commander, Major Weeber, was already missing, suspected dead, during the previous day's fighting, the last message from Bataillonstambour Belthle at the I. Bataillon HQ dugout being that one NCO and 17 men were still in position there, 'cut off and surrounded by English'. Known casualties for the day included at least three other officers and 129 men dead, wounded or missing. Among the captured were Assistenzarzt Spaich, and a number of orderlies and stretcher-bearers who remained with their injured charges when the British broke in. Only on the morning of 27 September was Leutnant Mayer, commander of 1. Kompagnie, able to state that, 'The overview now is that in second and third companies only a quarter of the establishment remains, in first and fourth, a third' (Vischer 1917: 53–55). Patrol leader Leutnant Mutschler added that the enemy were in possession of part of Hoher-Steg, this worry being relieved only by news that the Magdeburgers of Infanterie-Regiment Nr. 66 to the north were initiating a counter-attack (Vischer 1917: 53–55).

Despite their advantageous position, the men of 7th Bedfordshire were too close to the enemy for bombardment, so the attack was planned to begin as brisk 'waves' to storm the enemy 'with one rush', clearing them 'at the point of the bayonet'. As the war diary reported, 'At about 5.45 AM all was ready and a few minutes later the two lines advanced sweeping across the untaken portion of ground and trenches. Two M.Gs and a good deal of Rifle fire opened' (quoted in Deacon 2004: 56–57), with the result that 7th Bedfordshire went to ground, either in or short of the German trench. C Company led well on the right, but, according to the commanding

A British soldier rests during the battle of Thiepval Ridge. This man wears the 1908 Pattern web equipment usually issued to Regulars and Territorials. Other details include a mess-tin and his SMLE rifle complete with breech cover.

officer's report, D Company – which had taken longer to get into position – appears not to have got off the start line until about 0650hrs. 2/Lt Cartwright attacked with D Company:

> Up and over we went, and reaching the Hun front trench we halted. Captain Mulligan was hit at the start, so I took matters in hand. I looked at the lay of the land (it was here that my Platoon Sergeant named Hill, one of the very best, was killed by a sniper), and decided that if we reached the front line – our attack was in the nature of a wheeling movement – we should have reached our objective, so I sent Sergeants Wyatt and Slough with bombing parties down the trench. Immediately then a batch of some 30 Huns came out waving a white flag. These I sent back under Biggs to battalion headquarters and I regret I did not get as a souvenir a receipt for them. We made a flank attack along the trench, and Hill's death was avenged by Wyatt bayoneting the sniper.
>
> At last we came into touch with 'C' Company on the right, and how overjoyed I was to meet Captain L.H. Keep of 'C' Company, and knew that all was well. Then with another bombing party I went down to the left flank, and eventually came in touch with the Royal Fusiliers. They danced with joy to see us, having been there unsupported all through the night and I relieved their bombing post. Then I proceeded to clear the dug outs and reorganised the Company. Only Bobby Moyse and I were left. Potts had been hit immediately after I had left him, and a few days after he died of wounds. I chose my Company headquarters, and we were no sooner inside than two 5.9s hit the entrance, and Lance Corporal Fry, my runner, was slightly hurt. About noon Douggie came up, and took over command to my great relief … My Batman Dorrell was killed, and I often wonder if it was by reason of the fact that he was wearing a pair of my cast off breeches, and also carrying my walking stick, he having picked up the latter when I had thrown it down and armed myself with a rifle. Thus ended my first real battle … (Quoted in Deacon 2004: 119–20)

The worst hold-up was on the left, where 7th Bedfordshire's bombing officer, 22-year-old 2/Lt T.E. Adlam, rushed forward from shell hole to shell hole to help. He then got the men who had gone to ground to take out grenades and pull the pins, holding down the levers. On the command 'charge', he instructed them to rise simultaneously, run forward two or three yards and throw their bombs. This enabled them to scramble into the enemy trench. Here was exactly what they needed:

> We found bags of German bombs that looked like condensed milk cans on the top of sticks. On them was written '5 seks' so I experimented with one. I pulled the string and said, 'I'm going to count one, two, three, before I throw it'. My servant was beside me looking over the top of the trench and he said, 'bloody good shot sir, hit the bugger in the chest'. I think when the Germans found their own bombs coming back at them it rather put the wind up them. So the men brought armfuls of bombs along, and I just went gaily along, throwing these bombs and counting 'one, two, three' each time. It was most effective. Then we got to where the machine gun was, and I got a whole lot of bombs ready. I started throwing as fast as I could until my servant said, 'They're going, sir, they're going'. So I yelled, 'Come on Chaps, run in' and we charged up the trench. We never caught the

Germans, but we drove them out. Eventually we got to a certain point and the Commanding Officer saw two trenches leading up to the Schwaben Redoubt. And he said, 'It would be a good idea to get an advanced post up there'. So they started off and a man got killed straight away. I said, 'Oh, damn it. Let me go, I can do it', so I went on with some men and we bombed up the trench. We took more prisoners in dugouts and got our advance point out towards the enemy. (IWM: Sound 1974/35)

Adlam attributed his bombing skill and ability to hurl a grenade 40yd to the playing of cricket, and ambidextrous bowling – something that came in extremely useful when one arm was injured.

By 0925hrs the German position was desperate, as a report from Reserve-Leutnant Kimmich, commanding 2. Kompagnie, explained: 'I find myself, with the remains of the battalion – about 100 men – in the Hoher-Steg and the first and second line trenches of sector C5. The enemy are pressing on Hoher-Steg and are shooting at the garrison in the rear from Martinspfad. I will hold the Hoher-Steg as long as possible, but without support will be pressed into sector C4; close combat munitions running short' (quoted in Vischer 1917: 54). While the defence of Hoher-Steg bought the defenders time and a connection was made with Reserve-Infanterie-Regiment Nr. 77, Kimmich was gradually forced back on Marktgraben. Both food and water were running short. As he later recalled, 'Because of lack of hand grenades, I had to yield ground bit by bit in Hoher-Steg, but the barricade at the junction of Hoher-Steg and the front line trench was held in the face of constant attacks. Marktgraben was under heavy artillery fire all day long, so temporarily it was impossible to install a strong garrison there' (quoted in Vischer 1917: 54). So it was that they fell back from one trench block to another. Finally, remnants of I. Bataillon/Infanterie-Regiment Nr. 180 managed to escape along the trenches to the north and east, where the following day a sketch map showed them still assisting with the holding of Bulgarenweg.

A typical German *Stosstrupp* or shock troop, France, autumn 1916. From 1915 many ordinary infantry battalions began to form specialist assault groups. This team are equipped with grenades for which bags are worn over the shoulders, P 08 semi-automatic pistols, bayonets and trench knives. A few rifles or carbines were usually included to engage longer-range targets.

# The fight for Thiepval

On the morning of 27 September 1916, a lieutenant of 7th Bedfordshire, armed with a six-shot Webley revolver, directs a bombing party. Official British instructions, mindful of officer losses, directed that officers should not lead bombing parties; many did so, however, out of duty to their men, or when attacks stalled. The two bombers, wearing 'grenade waistcoats', throw into dugouts and over traverses after which 'bayonet men' will rush in to clear the area. To the right of the group can be seen a private soldier carrying reserves of Mills grenades in canvas 'bomb buckets'.

Despite inflicting casualties, the German garrison of I. Bataillon/Infanterie-Regiment Nr. 180 are seriously depleted, short of grenades, tired after their struggle with 12th Middlesex the previous day, and now threatened with encirclement.

**OPPOSITE**
German prisoners from the battle of Thiepval Ridge pictured in the *Daily Sketch*, 28 September 1916. A supplementary order, given three months earlier and supposed to be read to all ranks, had warned British troops to be on their guard against enemy 'ruses'. These included 'apparent' surrenders that were not genuine, and the fact that in transit, an MG 08 with a blanket thrown over it appeared like a stretcher. This was later denied to be an instruction to 'take no prisoners', and was probably intended to make men err on 'the safe side' rather than risk unnecessary casualties. Similar orders were found on the other side of the line, as for example at Thiepval, where the men of Oberst Alfred Vischer's Infanterie-Regiment Nr. 180 were reminded that the British soldier was 'daring and brave', only pretending to surrender, 'in order to take the next opportunity to stab his opponent to death with a knife'.

War reporter Philip Gibbs was on hand to give a sporting verdict for the *Daily Sketch*:

> Our men had to tackle an underground foe, who fired at them out of holes and crevices, while they remained hidden. They had to burrow for them, dive down into dark entries, fight in tunnels, get their hands about the throats of men who suddenly sprang up to them out of the earth … They gave us a good fight on land and underground, this garrison of Thiepval, and with a few exceptions they fought honourably, so that our men have no grudge against them now that they are prisoners of war.

The newspaper reported that '998 unwounded men and 40 wounded were brought down safely as prisoners, but others were killed on the way by their own barrage, and many fought until they died, so that some of the dugouts are filled with dead, and many lie above in the shell craters'. It was also claimed that a party of 16 Germans 'turned on the escort of two English soldiers taking them down, wounded them, and tried to go back to the fight. They had no mercy from other English soldiers who came up at this moment.' The credit, apparently, was due to the men of the New Armies, as the Germans were 'stupefied by the grim way in which our men attack. Reckless of loss, so that no barrage stops them, and they are amazed that men who were not soldiers a year ago should now be equal to their own best troops in fighting skill' (*Daily Sketch*: r/p 1916).

To crack Thiepval at last cost 7th Bedfordshire two officers and 110 men casualties, against which the battalion claimed 36 Germans captured 'and about 100 Germans killed by rifle fire and bayonets'. The war diary was not shy about the achievement: 'This action though apparently small, was of the utmost importance as without the whole of the Village of Thiepval and the trenches surrounding it being captured the whole line of attack was held up. So to the 7th Battalion, Bedfords (especially C and D Coys) belongs the honour and glory of the final destruction of one of the Germans' strongest positions and one which they had boasted could never be taken' (quoted in Deacon 2004: 56–57). Lt Cartwright was recommended for a Military Cross, which was not approved, but Lt Adlam was awarded the Victoria Cross for his actions at Thiepval, as his citation stated:

# DAILY SKETCH.

GUARANTEED DAILY NETT SALE MORE THAN 1,000,000 COPIES.

No. 2,358.      LONDON, THURSDAY, SEPTEMBER 28, 1916.     [Registered as a Newspaper.]     ONE HALFPENNY.

## STILL THEY COME!

"Between 3,000 and 4,000 Prisoners Have Been Taken in the Past 48 Hours."—*Official.*

For most conspicuous bravery. A portion of a village which had defied capture had to be taken at all costs, to permit subsequent operations to develop. This minor operation came under very heavy machine-gun and rifle fire. Second Lieutenant Adlam, realising that time was all-important, rushed from shell-hole to shell-hole under heavy fire, collecting men for a sudden rush, and for this purpose also collected many enemy grenades. At this stage he was wounded in the leg, but nevertheless he was able to out-throw the enemy, and then seizing his opportunity, and in spite of his wound, he led a rush, captured the position and killed the occupants.

According to Reserve-Leutnant Kimmich, when I. Bataillon/Infanterie-Regiment Nr. 180 was finally withdrawn from battle on 28 September, it was reduced to just three sections in strength; Kimmich was himself wounded. Despite great losses, they had fought 'an enemy hugely superior in numbers with fantastic courage'. Interesting evidence of the last stand of Infanterie-Regiment Nr. 180 would eventually be unearthed in 2003, when archaeological investigations, prior to the erection of the new visitor centre, turned up not just part of the chateau, but unexploded shells up to 9.2in calibre, ammunition, German grenades, parts of gas masks, and fittings for *Pickelhauben*. Human remains found in association with bits of German uniform included two fairly complete skeletons, one of which had a company button marked '5' or '3', and the other a harmonica and other personal effects.

# Analysis & Conclusion

Though some of the worst carnage of the Western Front lay in the future, by the time the Somme battle ended on 18 November 1916 it had become, to coin a German metaphor, a 'garden of the dead'. One modern estimate, put forward by Professor Hirschfeld, suggests that the British lost 419,654, the French 204,353, and the Germans about 465,000 total casualties – wounded, missing and prisoners as well as dead. We can be certain that most of these were infantrymen, and that artillery caused a majority of them.

While the shortcomings of the British artillery have received much attention, it should not be forgotten that German guns, if kept silent until the vital moment of the infantry onslaught, could reduce any Entente scheme to nought. A strong and well-placed defending barrage, correctly timed, as at Serre, would mean the numbers getting through were too small to have any chance of success. A barrage that fell between an attack and its lines of support, as at Guillemont, could effectively prevent both reinforcement and communication. Failures of communication affected both sides, but were most catastrophic when it proved impossible to end attacks that had clearly failed, or to reinforce those that were succeeding. Battlefield radio was gradually developed, but even by November 1918 had not reached a stage at which it was sufficiently light, durable and reliable to be carried forward with the first waves of attacking infantry. Both sides relied mainly on cables and field telephones for communication in fixed positions, but when leaving the trenches were reduced to the methods of the previous century: signal flags, runners, pigeons, flares and heliographs. Often messages arrived late, in the wrong order, or not at all. Above the level of the infantry company, command decisions might be given catastrophically late.

Both sides continued to fight for possession of tiny villages – never of any great strategic significance – long after they had ceased to be anything but rubble and a name on a map, and what had taken months to conquer would be lost in days during the German Spring Offensive of 1918. However, if the bigger Entente objective was to save Verdun by relieving pressure on the French, the battle had in fact been won during July. Conversely, if Haig really aimed at breakthrough, he was to be sadly disappointed. The German Army was badly battered, and fell back to the Hindenburg Line early in 1917, but this was controlled retirement to a shortened line.

# LESSONS LEARNED: THE BRITISH

For the British infantry, the first few days of battle revealed both appalling errors and great strengths. As one German report observed:

> During individual battles, which quickly developed because of our counter attack of 1 July against the Schwaben Redoubt, the general situation and later clearance of British pockets of resistance, the British soldiers displayed great courage, coolness under fire and a striking reluctance to take cover. Their main strength in this type of fighting was their masterly use of grenades, with which they were evidently trained with sporting enthusiasm and their numerous machine guns. Co-operation between hand grenade throwers, weapons carriers and grenade carrying parties was designed and organised down to the last detail. The enemy never seemed to run short of grenades. They generally gave up their nests if they perceived themselves to be threatened from several sides simultaneously. In this case they sometimes sought escape by running back across country without stopping, but on other occasions they withdrew slowly, fighting continuously. We actually observed the first during the battles of 1st July when, in the final phase of our attack on the Schwaben Redoubt, the pressure exerted by our numerically inferior assault groups was such that it almost induced panic among the very much stronger enemy. The other method was seen during the battles to clear the enemy out of the sections of the trench which the British still held after 1st July. There were no fundamental differences between the Ulster soldiers engaged on 1st July and the Yorkshiremen between 3 and 7 July.

As a German report on the events of July explained, the British had learned much, but still suffered problems of command:

> The English infantry has undoubtedly learnt much since the autumn [1915] offensive. It shows great dash in the attack, a factor to which immense confidence in its overwhelming artillery probably greatly contributes. The Englishman also has his physique and training in his favour. Commanders, however, in difficult situations, showed that they were not yet equal to their tasks. The men lost their heads and surrendered if they thought they were cut off. It was most striking how the enemy assembled and brought up large bodies of troops in close order into our zone of fire. The losses caused by our artillery fire were consequently large. One must, however, acknowledge the skill with which the English rapidly consolidated captured positions. The English infantry showed great tenacity in defence. This was especially noticeable in the case of small parties, which, when established with machine guns in the corner of a wood or group of houses, were very difficult to drive out. (General Staff 1916a)

By August much of the rigidity of thinking expressed in *Training of Divisions* was starting to disappear. Haig now spoke in favour of the use of small

Bloodied but unbowed, July 1916: 'Well done, the New Army'. The Somme was initially presented as a British victory, but half a century after 1916, British historian A.J.P. Taylor would refer to the Somme as an 'unredeemed defeat', setting the picture 'by which future generations saw the war: brave, helpless soldiers; blundering obstinate generals; nothing achieved. After the Somme men decided that the war would go on forever' (quoted in Philpott 2009: 592). Another half-century on, revisionists conclude that it was a worthwhile 'sacrifice' or even a 'Bloody Victory'. Participants were far more cautious, and complex, in their assessment.

WELL DONE, THE NEW ARMY

detachments, Lewis guns, and fewer men in the front line. It has been widely suggested that the Somme was a milestone, or even a turning point, on a tactical 'learning curve' for the British Army. Certainly the Somme led to improvements: in night attacks, raids, creeping barrages, shells, fuses, machine-gun tactics, deployments and use of the tank. As of February 1917 the infantry company was reorganized so that its platoons contained sections of riflemen, bombers, rifle-bombers and Lewis gunners. With this integration of 'all the weapons with which the infantry soldier is armed' the idea of sections supporting each other became far more practical. But none of this was smooth or predictable advance: methods and materials advanced in short bursts, often one step back and two forward, in a dance of death with an enemy who also improved in tactical skill with the progress of time.

## LESSONS LEARNED: THE GERMANS

To a significant degree the Germans fell into error by sacrificing lives to hold territory, as they had fewer lives but more territory to spare. As Prince Rupprecht, commander of the *Armeegruppe* that bore his name from late August 1916, commented, 'Hitherto our infantry had been inferior to that of the enemy in numerical terms, but in quality it had been superior. Now the heavy losses, and especially those among the officers and NCOs, has reduced this qualitative advantage to a considerable degree'. Counter-attacks were often successful on a local level, but also costly. As Ludendorff later explained:

> Without doubt [the German infantry] fought too doggedly, clinging to the mere holding of ground, with the result that losses were heavy. The conspicuous lines of trenches, which appeared as sharp lines on every aerial photograph, supplied far too good a target for enemy artillery. The whole system of defence had to be made broader, looser, and better adapted to the ground. (Ludendorff 1919: 323)

Despite its shortcomings, the Germans were clearly shocked by the Entente artillery and what it could do, bombardment being 'almost continuous and of a volume never before experienced'. Previous instructions tended to take for granted the existence of trenches, but on many parts of the Somme front these ceased to exist. Accordingly, it was recommended that future training should focus on self-reliance, crossing ground that is being shelled, defence of shell holes and use of all types of hand grenades and machine guns. For attacking, 'attacks by sectors, according to time table, following up close to our barrage' were to be used, but also the men were to be trained in the

> … rapid execution of counter attacks over open ground under different conditions. Bombers in front, skirmishers about 10 metres behind them, a small number of bodies in support slightly further in rear. In wooded country these move in file, otherwise in extended order … One of the most important lessons drawn from the battle of the Somme is that, under heavy, methodical artillery fire, the front should be only thinly held, but by reliable men and a few machine guns, even when there is always a possibility of a hostile attack. When this was not done, the casualties were so great before the enemy's attack was launched, that the possibility of the

front line repulsing the attack by its own efforts was very doubtful. The danger of the front line being rushed when so lightly held must be overcome by placing supports (infantry and machine guns), distributed in groups according to the ground, as close as possible behind the foremost fighting line. Their task is to rush forward to reinforce the front line at the moment the enemy attacks, without waiting for orders from the rear …

The detailing of assaulting parties in an attack has proved very useful. Their chief advantage lay in the freshness of the specially selected personnel who had not been engaged in previous fighting … They felt that they were a body of elite troops, which indeed they proved themselves to be. (General Staff 1916a)

The hand grenade was thought to be the 'most important infantry weapon both in attack and defence'; accordingly, it was recommended not only that numbers be increased, but that they should be rationalized into one type. This was not, of course, achieved. However, the idea of 'shock troops', combined with a weakening of the tyranny of the line, greater self-reliance and greater integration of weapons systems at the lowest-possible tactical level did point the way to the future.

Much would be made of the idea of the Sommekampfer, holding out against the odds. There was even a film – *Bei Unseren Helden an der Somme* (*With our Heroes on the Somme*) – produced in answer to the British film *Battle of the Somme*. Yet, practically speaking, the German High Command recognized that the blood of the best of the Kaiser's infantry was no fair exchange for holding an advanced front line offering few strategic advantages. Accordingly, the German Army retired to the more viable *Siegfriedstellung* – the Hindenburg Line – in March 1917.

'Remnants of the Somme fighters': German machine-gunners pose with an MG 08 in the winter snow of 1916. One area in which the German infantry clearly felt outclassed was light machine guns, for while small numbers of Madsen weapons were used there was no general issue of light machine guns to the companies of the line. Improvised light 'trench mounts' proved their worth, but could never turn the MG 08 into a mobile battlefield support weapon to match the Lewis gun.

# UNIT ORGANIZATIONS

## British infantry battalion

The British infantry battalion 'War Establishment' was 977 men, plus 30 officers – although on campaign these numbers could be much reduced – and fighting strength was more like 800 once specialists were discounted. It was typically commanded by a lieutenant-colonel, with a major as second-in-command and three officers serving as adjutant (dealing with administration), quartermaster (handling transport and supplies) and medical officer (attached from the Royal Army Medical Corps). Other officers were allotted responsibilities such as 'Bombing' or 'Intelligence'. The regimental sergeant-major was primarily responsible for discipline. Other NCOs and men held responsibilities for various roles such as signals, transport and maintenance of weapons.

The four companies, each commanded by a major or captain, each totalled 221 men and six officers at full strength. A captain or lieutenant acted as second-in-command, and was assisted by a company sergeant-major and six soldiers. Companies were normally given letters – typically A to D. The company was divided in turn into four platoons. Each platoon, was commanded by a lieutenant or 2nd lieutenant assisted by one or two sergeants and included four 12-man sections, each typically led by a corporal. In battle sections were usually eight to ten strong, and losses forced many officers to be 'acting' at a higher level than their 'substantive' rank.

All soldiers and NCOs (except some specialists) carried rifles and bayonets; on the eve of the battle of the Somme official allocation of Lewis guns doubled to 16 per battalion, meaning (in theory) that one could be fielded by every infantry platoon. By mid-1916 the Vickers guns initially integral to each infantry battalion had been withdrawn and assigned to specialist machine-gun companies, one per infantry brigade. Although every British infantry battalion was part of a parent regiment, in practice it would nearly always serve alongside battalions of other regiments in a four-battalion infantry brigade; there were three such brigades in each infantry division at the time of the Somme battles. The division also included a pioneer battalion.

## German infantry battalion

At the time of the Somme battles the average German infantry battalion was – at least in theory – organized in much the same way as it had been in 1914. Unlike its British counterpart, the German infantry battalion normally served alongside two others in a regiment that acted as its parent unit in a specific, tactical sense. Each three-battalion regiment had its own regimental staff. Although the German infantry division had included two infantry brigades at the outbreak of war, by 1916 it was increasingly common for a single, three-regiment infantry brigade to be fielded by each division, making a total of nine infantry battalions per division. Of course in confused piecemeal fighting on the Somme, individual battalions – or even parts – could sometimes be detached from their parent regiments and assigned to a different, temporary formation.

Nominally each German infantry battalion fielded 1,080 men, 26 of whom were officers. By 1916 the battalion commander was theoretically a *Major* but sometimes a *Hauptmann*, as the German Army – unlike the British – had no system of acting ranks, and awarded officer rank very sparingly. Extensive use was made, however, of 'deputy officers' and various grades of senior NCO to lead platoons. Each *Kompagnie*, usually led by an *Oberleutnant* or a *Leutnant*, fielded three *Züge* (platoons). Although in theory the *Kompagnie* was made up of 265 men including five officers, this number was normally much reduced by July 1916. Each *Zug*, notionally 80 men strong, comprised four *Korporalschaften*, each led by an NCO. Each *Korporalschaft* was divided into two *Gruppen*, the smallest tactical unit comprising eight men and a *Gefreiter*.

As with the British, the vast majority of soldiers carried the bolt-action rifle; the MG 08/15, the German Army's response to the British Lewis, only appeared in significant quantities in 1917. Initially six MG 08 machine guns were fielded by each infantry regiment deployed in a 13th, independent company alongside the regiment's three rifle battalions, although individual machine-gun teams could be subordinated to local infantry commanders. By the time of the Somme these guns were supplemented by independent *Maschinengewehr-Scharfschützen-Truppen* (machine-gun sharpshooter troops), additional weapons, or a second MG company. Though few and far between, *Musketen-Bataillonen* also existed, armed with light machine guns. During the battle the number of machine guns fielded by the regimental company increased, and on 26 September 1916 it was ordered to be split into three to provide each infantry battalion with its own, integral machine-gun company.

# ORDERS OF BATTLE

## Serre, 1 July 1916

### 94th Brigade (Brig-Gen H.C. Rees)
11th (Service) Battalion (Accrington), The East Lancashire Regiment
12th (Service) Battalion (Sheffield), The York and Lancaster Regiment
13th (Service) Battalion (Barnsley), The York and Lancaster Regiment
14th (Service) Battalion (Barnsley), The York and Lancaster Regiment

Both 93rd and 94th Brigades of 31st Division were in the attack, while 92nd Brigade was in reserve. Rees's brigade also included 94th Company, Machine Gun Corps, and 94th Trench Mortar Battery; divisional assets included four artillery brigades, four trench-mortar batteries and a pioneer battalion.

### 9. Badisches Infanterie-Regiment Nr. 169 (Major von Struensee)
Part of 52. Division and under the command of 104. Infanterie-Brigade, Struensee's regiment deployed I. Bataillon on the British 94th Brigade front, with close support from III. Bataillon. Divisional assets included two field artillery regiments, one heavy artillery battalion and a *Pionier* (engineer) company.

## Guillemont, 30 July 1916

### 90th Brigade (Brig-Gen C.J. Steavenson)
2nd Battalion, The Royal Scots Fusiliers
16th (Service) Battalion, The Manchester Regiment
17th (Service) Battalion, The Manchester Regiment
18th (Service) Battalion, The Manchester Regiment

Also deploying 90th Company, Machine Gun Corps, and 90th Trench Mortar Battery, 90th Brigade was one of three infantry brigades in 30th Division, alongside 21st Brigade and 89th Brigade. 30th Division's assets included four brigades of artillery, four trench-mortar batteries, and a pioneer battalion.

### German forces occupying front-line trenches
I. Bataillon/Königlich Bayerisches 22. Reserve-Infanterie-Regiment (three companies with attached machine guns forward, one company in support)

### Available German counter-attack forces
Königliche Sächsische Reserve-Infanterie-Regiment Nr. 104 (three battalions and machine-gun company, with Maschinengewehr-Scharfschützen-Trupp Nr. 197 attached)
Königliche Sächsische Reserve Infanterie Regiment Nr. 107 (three battalions and machine-gun company)

Königliche Sächsische Reserve-Infanterie-Regiment Nr. 133 (three battalions, plus Feld-Maschinengewehr-Züge Nrs. 180, 181 and 191)
Königliche Sächsische Reserve-Jäger-Bataillon Nr. 13 (with Feld-Maschinengewehr-Zug Nr. 385)
Sächsisches Sturm-Kompanie (formed from divisional personnel)

In the event not all the Saxon troops were committed. 24 Reserve-Division's infantry assets were deployed under 48. Reserve-Infanterie-Brigade, and were supported by a cavalry squadron, two companies of *Pioniere*, a *Minenwerfer* company and two artillery regiments. The bulk of 24. Reserve-Division was held back in the second and third lines; its order of battle here is as given for 14 July (Stosch: 1927; see also D. Rottgardt (2007), *German Divisions in World War I Vol. 3*, West Chester, PA: The Nafziger Collection, pp. 79–82).

## Thiepval, 26–27 September 1916

### Initial British attack, 26 September
### 53rd Brigade (Brig-Gen H.W. Higginson)
8th (Service) Battalion, The Norfolk Regiment
8th (Service) Battalion, The Suffolk Regiment
10th (Service) Battalion, The Essex Regiment
6th (Service) Battalion, Princess Charlotte of Wales's (Royal Berkshire Regiment)
### 54th Brigade (Brig-Gen T.H. Shoubridge)
11th (Service) Battalion, The Royal Fusiliers (City of London Regiment)
7th (Service) Battalion, The Bedfordshire Regiment
6th (Service) Battalion, The Northamptonshire Regiment
12th (Service) Battalion, The Duke of Cambridge's Own (Middlesex Regiment)

Each of 18th (Eastern) Division's three infantry brigades included a machine-gun company and a trench-mortar battery. Divisional assets included four brigades of artillery, four trench-mortar batteries and a pioneer battalion. On 26 September the main British attack was supported by fire from 49th (West Riding) Division to the west of the village, and two tanks were used.

### German defenders of Thiepval
10. Württembergisches Infanterie-Regiment Nr. 180 (three battalions with two machine-gun companies and attached mortars)
Reserve-Infanterie-Regiment Nr. 77 (elements)

26. Reserve-Division assets included a cavalry squadron, an artillery regiment and an artillery battalion, two *Pionier* companies and a trench-mortar company.

# BIBLIOGRAPHY

## Published works

Anonymous (1923). *Sixteenth, Seventeenth, Eighteenth, Nineteenth Battalions, The Manchester Regiment.* Manchester: Sherratt & Hughes.

Barton, Peter (2006). *The Somme: A New Panoramic Perspective.* London: Constable.

Beckett, Ian F.W. & Simpson, K., eds (1985). *A Nation in Arms.* Manchester: Manchester University Press.

Bond, Brian (2002). *The Unquiet Western Front.* Cambridge: Cambridge University Press.

Brennert, Hans (1917). *Bei Unseren Helden an der Somme.* Berlin: Eysler.

Bucher, Georg (2006). *In the Line, 1914–1918.* Uckfield: Naval & Military Press.

Bull, Stephen (2007). *Stosstrupptaktik: German Assault Troops of the First World War.* Stroud: Spellmount.

Deacon, M.G., ed. (2004). *The Shiny Seventh: The Seventh (Service) Battalion Bedfordshire Regiment at War.* Bedfordshire Historical Record Society, Vol. 83. Woodbridge: Boydell.

Duffy, Christopher (2006). *Through German Eyes: The British and the Somme, 1916.* London: Weidenfeld & Nicolson.

Edmonds, Charles (1929). *A Subaltern's War.* London: Peter Davies.

Garwood, John M. (1992). *The Chorley Pals.* Manchester: N. Richardson.

General Staff (1916a). *Experiences of the IV German Corps in the Battle of the Somme During July, 1916.* SS478; translation of a German document.

General Staff (1916b). *Lessons Drawn from the Battle of the Somme by Stein's Group.* SS480; translation of a German document.

General Staff (1916c). *Notes on German Army Corps XIV Reserve Corps and 52nd Division.* SS394.

General Staff (1916d). *Training of Divisions for Offensive Action.* SS109.

Gibbs, Philip (1917). *The Germans on the Somme.* London: Darling & Son.

Griffith, Paddy (1994). *Battle Tactics of the Western Front.* New Haven, CT: Yale University Press.

Haig, Sir Douglas, ed. Gary Sheffield & John Bourne (2005). *War Diaries and Letters 1914–1918.* London: Weidenfeld & Nicolson.

Hart, Peter (2005). *The Somme.* London: Cassell.

Hirschfeld, Gerhard, et al. (2006). *Die Deutschen an der Somme.* Essen: Klartext.

Holmes, Richard (2005). *Tommy: The British soldier on the Western Front 1914–1918.* London: Harper Perennial.

Immanuel, Friedrich (1912). *Lehnerts Handbuch für den Truppenführer.* Berlin: Mittler.

Jackson, A., trans. (originally 1924). *Festschrift zum 1. Regimentstag des ehem. 8. Bad. Inf.-Reg. Nr169 in Lahr am 30. und 31. August 1924.*

Jackson, A. (2013). *Accrington's Pals: The Full Story.* Barnsley: Pen & Sword.

Lais, Otto (1935). *Erlebnisse Badischer Frontsoldaten, Band 1: Maschinengewehre im Eisernen Regiment (8. Badisches Infanterie-Regiment Nr. 169).* Karlsruhe: G. Braun.

Levine, Joshua, ed. (2008). *Forgotten Voices of the Somme.* London: Ebury.

Liddle, Peter H. (1992). *The 1916 Battle of the Somme: A Reappraisal.* London: Leo Cooper.

Ludendorff, Erich von (1919). *Ludendorff's Own Story.* New York: Harper.

Macdonald, Lyn (1983). *Somme.* London: Michael Joseph.

Merkatz, Friedrich von (1918). *Das Maschinengewehr 08.* Berlin: Eisenschmidt.

Middlebrook, Martin (1984). *The First Day on the Somme.* London: Penguin.

Miles, Wilfrid (1938). *Military Operations France and Belgium, 1916.* Official History, Vol. II. London: HMSO.

Philpott, William (2009). *Bloody Victory: The Sacrifice on the Somme and the Making of the Twentieth Century.* London: Little, Brown.

Powell, Anne, ed. & trans. (2006). *The Fierce Light: The Battle of the Somme. Prose and Poetry.* Stroud: Sutton.

Rabenau, Kurt von (1915). *Dienstunterricht des Deutschen Pioniers.* Berlin: Eisenschmidt.

Schreibershofen, Max von (1914). *Die Modernen Waffen. Wissenswertes für Jedermann über die Verteidigungsmittel im Gegenwärtigen Kriege.* Leipzig: Verlagsbuchhandlung Curt Stück.

Schulz, Otto (1915). *Dienstunterricht des Bayerischen Infanteristen.* Berlin: Bossische.

Sheldon, Jack (2005). *The German Army on the Somme.* Barnsley: Pen & Sword.

Sheldon, Jack (2006). *The Germans at Thiepval.* Barnsley: Pen & Sword.

Simkins, Peter (1988). *Kitchener's Army.* Manchester: Manchester University Press.

Spencer, Tony, ed. (2008). *Stanley Spencer's Great War Diary.* Barnsley: Pen & Sword.

Stedman, Michael (1998). *Guillemont: Somme.* Barnsley: Pen & Sword.

Stedman, Michael (2004). *Manchester Pals.* Barnsley: Leo Cooper.

Stosch, Albrecht von, ed. (1927). *Somme Nord, 2 Teil.* Berlin: Reichsarchiv.

Turner, William (1993). *Pals: The 11th (Service) Battalion (Accrington) The East Lancashire Regiment.* Barnsley: Wharncliffe.

Ulrich, Bernd, et al. (2010). *German Soldiers in the Great War.* Barnsley: Pen & Sword.

US War Office (1917a). *Notes on the German Army in War.* Washington, DC: War Department.

US War Office (1917b). *Notes on the Use of Machine Guns in Trench Warfare.* Washington, DC: Army War College.

US War Office (1918). *German Notes on Minor Tactics.* Washington, DC: War Department.

Vischer, Alfred (1917). *Das 10. Wüerttemberg Infanterie Regiment No 180 in der Somme Schlacht, 1916.* Stuttgart: Uhlandschen.

Westlake, Ray (1994). *British Battalions on the Somme.* Barnsley: Leo Cooper.

Wurmb, Eckart von (1908). *Dienstunterricht des Deutschen Infanteristen.* Berlin: R. Eisenschmidt.

## Newspapers

*Daily Sketch,* reprinted 1916
*Manchester Guardian,* 1916

## Archival sources

**Accrington Library:**
Bill Turner Collection.

**Duke of Lancaster's Regiment Museum, Fulwood:**
War Diary 11th (Service) Battalion (Accrington), East Lancashire Regiment.

**Imperial War Museum, London:**
Documents 11098: *Private papers of P.J. Kennedy.*
Documents 77/179/1: *Private papers of Brig-Gen H.C. Rees.*
Sound 1974/35: *Interview with T.C. Adlam.*

**Generallandesarchiv, Karlsruhe:**
456-EV-42 Vol. 127: *The Heroic Deeds of the 6th Company, 169th Infantry Regiment in the Battles at Serre.*

**War Diaries, The National Archives, London:**
WO 95/2339/3: 30th Division.
WO 95/2340: 90th Brigade.
WO 95/2339/3: 18th Battalion Manchester Regiment.
WO 95/2044: 12th Battalion Middlesex Regiment.

**North West Sound Archive, Clitheroe:**
Recollections of Will Marshall.

# INDEX

References to illustrations are shown in **bold**.
References to plates are shown in **bold** with
caption pages in brackets, e.g. **68–69** (70).